FAT LOSER!
MENTAL TOUGHNESS FOR DIETERS

Steve Siebold

FAT LOSER!
MENTAL TOUGHNESS FOR DIETERS

Steve Siebold

Published by London House
www.londonhousepress.com

©2014 by Steve Siebold
All Rights Reserved. Printed in the United States.

No part of this book may be reproduced, stored in or introduced into a retrieval system, or transmitted, in any form or by any means – electronic, mechanical, photocopying, recording or otherwise – without the prior written permission of the copyright owner.

Ordering Information
To order additional copies visit
www.fatloser.com or call 561-733-9078

ISBN: 978-0-9755003-9-2

Credits

Book Design by Sandra Smith Larson

DEDICATION

This book is dedicated to the pioneers of the Think Rich Team.

Together, we're going to help ten million people get healthier and create 1,000 million-dollar coaches along the way.

Thank you for your loyalty, dedication and persistence.

CONTENTS

DEDICATION 3
COMPLY OR DIE 9
EAT FOR ENERGY 12
EAT FOR SEX 15
EAT FOR MONEY 18
EAT FOR THE FUTURE 21
SAY NO 24
STOP CARING WHAT FAT PEOPLE THINK 27
STOP WAITING TO BE RESCUED 30
EAT STRATEGICALLY 33
EMBRACE HUNGER 36
BEGIN SUFFERING 39
DETERMINE THE PRICE 42
STOP DELUDING YOURSELF 45
GROW UP EMOTIONALLY 48
REMEMBER FAT SICKENS AND KILLS 51
STOP LETTING YOURSELF OFF THE HOOK 54
STOP MAKING EXCUSES 57
WORK HARDER ON YOU THAN ON YOUR DIET 60
STOP STARTING OVER 63
BEGIN STARING 66
STOP LISTENING TO DOCTORS 69
STOP MAKING WEIGHT LOSS COMPLEX 72
START PRIORITIZING EXERCISE 75

SHORE UP YOUR BALANCE SHEET	78
STOP WHINING AND START SUCCEEDING	81
EMBRACE EMOTIONAL SUPPORT	84
ACCEPT REALITY	87
STOP BEHAVING LIKE A CHILD	90
BEGIN COMPARTMEN-TALIZING	93
STOP ACTING FAT	97
STOP SOCIALIZING WITH FAT PEOPLE	100
BEGIN KEEPING YOUR WORD	103
BECOME COMMITTED	106
ANALYZE YOUR BELIEFS	109
STOP BEING STUPID	112
BEGIN DELAYING GRATIFICATION	115
SEE YOURSELF AS A COMEBACK ARTIST	118
BEGIN BEING COACHABLE	121
STOP TALKING AND START WORKING	124
DO THE WORK	127
EMBRACE THE DISCIPLINE	130
BEGIN DOING THE WORK IT TAKES TO SUCCEED	133
BEGIN BELIEVING IN YOURSELF	136
FOCUS ON THE FUTURE	139
EAT CONGRUENTLY	142
LISTEN TO FIT PEOPLE	145
DIET FOR FUN	148
DIET FOR PROFIT	151
FORGIVE YOURSELF	154
KNOW YOUR WHY	157

BECOME OBSESSED WITH SUCCESS	160
BUILD NEW HABITS	163
BECOME HAPPY THROUGH FITNESS	166
BECOME BRUTALLY HONEST WITH YOURSELF	169
WRITE ABOUT YOUR BODY VISION	172
DEMAND LOGICAL THINKING	175
STOP EGO-BASED THINKING	178
GO TO WAR	181
THINK FOR YOURSELF	184
BE A ROLE MODEL	187
BE POSITIVE	190
EMBRACE MOMENTUM	193
BUILD A TEAM	196
EMBRACE CHANGE	199
USE FAILURE AS FUEL	202
EXPECT EXTRA BENEFITS	205
GET ORGANIZED	208
EXPECT PEACE OF MIND	211
EMBRACE PERSISTENCE	214
PAY THE PRICE	217
FOCUS ON RESULTS	220
BECOME MENTALLY TOUGH	223
BUILD SELF-ESTEEM	226
MONITOR YOUR VIBRATION	229
REWARD EXECUTION	232
EMBRACE RECOGNITION	235
PROGRAM YOURSELF FOR SUCCESS	238

CONTINUE TO LEARN	241
BEWARE OF YOUR EMOTIONAL REACTIONS	244
KNOW THE CLOCK IS TICKING	247
MAKE FITNESS SIMPLE	250
EMBRACE SELF-RELIANCE	253
EMBRACE SEXUAL ENERGY	256
GET EXCITED	259
NEVER SAY DIE	262
FOLLOW ROLE MODELS	265
STOP SAYING DIETS DON'T WORK	268
RADIATE SUCCESS	271
BECOME DESENSITIZED	274
KNOW YOUR BELIEF IS NOT REQUIRED	277
TAKE PRIDE IN YOUR BODY	280
CELEBRATE WEIGHT LOSS	284
DON'T BELIEVE PROPAGANDA	288
THINK CRITICALLY	291
STOP APPROVAL ADDICTION	294
STOP WHINING	297
BEGIN DIETING FOR LIFE	300
START CELEBRATING	303
START MOTIVATING	306
EMBRACE YOUR SUCCESS	309
GUARD THE DOOR	312
LEARNING RESOURCES	315
ABOUT THE AUTHOR	328

MENTAL-TOUGHNESS STRATEGY #1

COMPLY OR DIE

Don't fall into the psychological trap of the masses thinking you can be ninety-nine percent compliant on your diet and succeed. You may be able to cheat a little when you become fit, but in the beginning, you must commit to all-out massive action. Success is about sticking to the goal, no matter what it takes. Imagine informing your spouse that you've been ninety-nine percent faithful in your marriage. You wouldn't be shocked at the incredulous reaction, yet we've been brainwashed to believe diets are different. They're not.

Success in any endeavor requires a hundred percent commitment, which is the reason most people don't succeed. Short cuts never work, and the consciousness that searches for them will destroy your results in other areas of life as well. If you're fat and want to be fit, comply fully or resolve to struggle with extra weight for the rest of your life. If you're obese and want to survive, comply or die. It's not pretty, but it is simple. The fat person's belief that you can beat the system by altering it is delusional. No one goes from fat to fit without a hundred percent commitment. You don't try to diet; you diet. If you play the middle ground, it will only end in frustration, disappointment, and resentment. A full commitment will take you to the promised land of health and happiness.

Guarantee your success by planning your meals in advance to minimize temptation. Set a goal to be one hundred percent compliant for thirty consecutive days and give yourself a non-edible reward for achieving it. Re-evaluate after thirty days and commit to full compliance for another thirty days. Three successful thirty-day sessions of complete dietary compliance and you will never be the same. Not only will you drop the weight, you'll begin to believe you can do anything, and you'll be right.

"Don't delude yourself into thinking you can beat the system. If you could, you would have done it by now."

Critical Thinking Question

ARE YOU REALLY PREPARED TO COMMIT TO ONE HUNDRED PERCENT COMPLIANCE ON YOUR DIET FOR THE NEXT THIRTY DAYS?

Action Step

List the five biggest reasons why you must lose weight in the next thirty days.

MENTAL-TOUGHNESS STRATEGY #2

EAT FOR ENERGY

Energy is life, and dragging excess fat around drains your physical, emotional, and spiritual energy. The implications of this energy depletion cannot be overstated. Low energy costs you time, money, relationships, and most important, enjoyment of life. Being tired all the time sucks, and fat people spend their days feeling sluggish, sloppy, and sleepy. It's all bad. The solution is to focus on eating for energy instead of pleasure. You don't need a nutritionist to tell you what foods to eat to maximize your energy levels. You've been eating your whole life, and you know what works for you. Knowing isn't the issue, it's doing something about it that requires mental toughness. Increasing your awareness regarding which foods boost your energy and which ones foods drain it is the first step. Everyone is different, but I know when I eat bread, my body creates excess acid and has to expend more energy trying to regain balance. Steak slows me down and turkey makes me tired. On the other side, salad keeps me light on my feet, greens help me think more clearly, and cellular cleansing keeps me sharp. You know your body better than any doctor or nutritionist, and you know when you're filling it with energy- producing or energy-depleting foods.

We all want more energy, so why do we eat foods that drain it? Because we all love the instant pleasure of fine-tasting foods, many of which extract far more energy than they're worth. The energy costs of poor-food choices are substantial, including the energy-robber of guilt feelings that are generated from knowingly eating self-destructive foods. It's a vicious cycle, and the answer lies in improving your decision-making when it comes to food choices.

FAT LOSER!

The habit of making food choices that serve your best interests will become easier every day. The secret centers on thinking about it before every meal, weighing both the energy costs of poor-food choices and the energy benefits of nutritious ones. In thirty days of disciplined thinking, you'll develop the habit of making food selections that serve your best interests and supply you with abundant energy. And you'll enhance your self-esteem and self-confidence in the process.

"Energy is life, and the more you have, the happier you'll be. Food fuels your energy and determines how much you have. Make food choices that boost your energy and you'll live a happier, more healthful, more successful life."

Critical Thinking Question

ARE YOU CHOOSING THE INSTANT PLEASURE OF NON-NUTRITIOUS FOODS OVER THE EXPERIENCE OF ABUNDANT PHYSICAL, EMOTIONAL, AND SPIRITUAL ENERGY?

Action Step

Begin rating your food choices on the energy scale of 1-7, 7 as the foods creating the most energy and 1 as the foods draining you.

MENTAL-TOUGHNESS STRATEGY #3

EAT FOR SEX

When I wrote my best-selling book *Die Fat or Get Tough: 101 Differences in Thinking between Fat People and Fit People*, I had no idea the anger it was going to generate in the general public. After Kathie Lee Gifford interviewed me on *The Today Show*, I received three death threats. When I appeared on the BBC in London, they insisted on surrounding me with security guards.

Holding people responsible for their own results is risky business, and probably the reason most authors, physicians, and fitness gurus tell people that outside sources are to blame. I refuse to do that because as a mental-toughness coach, it goes against everything I teach. One of the most controversial areas of weight loss is its relationship to sex. The reality states that fat is ugly, diminishes sex drive, and turns partners off. I've made this statement in the press during hundreds of interviews worldwide and it infuriates people. Even the reporters become angry, although I've noticed it's only the newspaper, magazine, and radio reporters who become really upset. The television anchors are mostly positive and believe in the message. Of course, these people are typically physical specimens who work out regularly and watch every bit of food they put in their mouths. The television-viewing public wants to see fit, attractive people delivering the news, not fat people looking like they're going to explode on the air. Americans expect their TV reporters to be smart and sexy; and most of the successful ones are.

Being fat will damage your sex life, and if you're really fat, it will destroy it. Spouses and partners who tell you being fat doesn't matter are lying, and while they're only trying to avoid hurting you, they are *still* lying. Excessive fat is ugly, disgusting, and the ultimate anti-sex condition. The answer lies in eating for sex, which means considering the cost to your sex life every time you make a food choice. People with lean, fit, healthy bodies are the most sexually attractive and all of us are capable of achieving this goal. A better body equals better sex. A better body attracts better sex partners. A better body makes us feel sexier and puts us in the mood for sex. A better body is better all around when it comes to a healthful, satisfying sex life.

"People with fit bodies attract partners with fit bodies. Fit people enjoy better sex. If you like sex, don't get fat. If you're fat, become fit and better sex is on its way."

Critical Thinking Question

IF YOU WERE MORE FIT, WOULD YOU BE HAVING MORE SEX?

Action Step

Develop the habit of carefully considering the way every food choice will affect your sex life.

MENTAL-TOUGHNESS STRATEGY #4

EAT FOR MONEY

If you're fat, it's costing you a fortune. Employers aren't allowed to discriminate against you for being a blob, but they do anyway. Customers are supposed to hire or fire you based on your product or service and not on the way you look, but they don't. We're all taught not to judge a book by its cover, but we do. Welcome to the world. It's not perfect, but it's all we have, so instead of complaining about something you can't change, you might as well adapt to it and succeed within its framework.

Fat people are marginalized instantly in business for being unable to control something that isn't difficult to control. After all, if you can't control your most basic primal urge, how can I trust you with my business? You say you have an eating disorder? Stop reading and seek help. You say you're a food addict? Take a twelve-step program. You say you have emotional issues and use food as a drug? Get therapy. For the rest of us psychologically and physiologically healthy people, we need to grow up, get tough, and put away the pizza. Or, pay the price in the marketplace for being fat. It's that simple. Fat people lose out on business opportunities, promotions, and other financial advancements because they're perceived as being lazy, undisciplined, and unorganized, especially by fit people who prioritize their health and know that healthful eating and exercise regimens aren't difficult to follow.

Are their perceptions of fat people correct? Not always, but in the real world perceptions are reality, and the people with the gold make the rules. Another genuine concern of employers is the insurance costs and risks associated with hiring a fat person.

Obesity has been linked to every major disease from cancer to diabetes, and that means time off for treatment, excessive medical expenses, and higher insurance rates. Isn't it easier and less risky to hire a fit candidate? Yes, and that's what employers do. Can you honestly blame them? So the next time you're tempted to betray yourself with that hot fudge sundae or banana split, consider its cost to you financially and eat for money instead. Fish, whole grains, fruits, vegetables and other healthy choices are the money foods, so eat them instead of foods that drain your bank account and send you starving for opportunity. After all, how many rich fat people do you know?

"Winning is a habit. So is losing. Build the habit of disciplining yourself in these areas of life that matter, and be undisciplined in the areas that don't. Fitness matters. Money matters. Relationships matter. Determine the others and let the rest go."

Critical Thinking Question

DO YOU BELIEVE BEING FAT IS COSTING YOU MONEY OR ARE PEOPLE IN POWER BEYOND DISCRIMINATION?

Action Step

Add twenty-five percent to your annual income. That's probably the amount it's costing you in lost opportunity for being fat. **Start eating for a twenty-five percent pay raise today.**

MENTAL-TOUGHNESS STRATEGY #5

EAT FOR THE FUTURE

The masses want everything instantly. As a matter of fact, we *all* want everything instantly. We live in a microwave society where instant pleasure outweighs the benefits of delayed gratification. This is one of the primary causes of the obesity epidemic. I eat the pizza today and pay the price tomorrow. I purchase the luxury home today and my debt-level is devastated tomorrow. I watch TV instead of exercising today and I'm less healthy tomorrow. The promise of instant pleasure has a strong appeal, and most of us fall prey to its seduction. Fat losers don't. Winners always find a way to victory, and it lies in delayed gratification. Everything you eat falls into one of two categories: instant pleasure or delayed gratification. Every meal is an investment in your future or an up-front expenditure. Either you invest in yourself and secure your future or you divest your physiological portfolio and end up fat.

Fat people have a great deal in common with penniless people. Both are addicted to the psychological fix of emotional spending. Some are medicating themselves to mask emotional pain or to dull the impact of psychological scars and wounds. This is sad, but true. The bottom line is that everyone has scars, wounds, and emotional pain to some degree and overcoming it requires dealing with the pain and succeeding anyway. If your emotional or psychological pain is beyond this strategy and you need professional help, seek it. There's no shame in sickness. You need to be mentally tough enough to know when you need help. Don't feel bad. We all need help sometimes; it's part of being human. For the rest of us, however, avoiding the temptation of the instant, microwave mentality is the answer.

Children need things now. Adults are mature enough to wait. The benefits of delaying pleasure are substantial, and becoming a fat loser is only one of them. This mind-set becomes a habit, and habits are contagious. They carry over into every area of life. One day you start eating for the future and the next you begin investing for the future. And then you start applying the same strategy to your relationships. Giving an uncomfortable "I love you" today yields a more healthful relationship tomorrow. Nothing succeeds like success. It's both a habit and a way of life. Your future is waiting. Start eating for it.

"Fat people eat for the instant pleasure in the present. Fat losers eat for the delayed gratification of the future. One approach is childish and the other mature. Behaving like a child is a losing game, and it's the game most people play."

Critical Thinking Question

WHEN IT COMES TO YOUR DIET, ARE YOU BEHAVING LIKE A MATURE ADULT OR A SPOILED CHILD?

Action Step

Rate yourself on a scale of 1-7, 7, you eat like a mature adult and 1, you eat like a spoiled child.

MENTAL-TOUGHNESS STRATEGY #6

SAY NO

We're raised as children to show good manners and act politely. We learn that saying *please* and *thank you* can take us a long way. And if we possibly can, we try to say *yes* when people ask us favors. Many of us over-commit ourselves to things because we don't want to say *no* and disappoint others. We're trained to be people-pleasers, which means saying *yes* to things to which we should to be saying *no*. It's critical on your quest to becoming a fat loser to build the habit of saying *no, no* to unhealthful foods, *no* to laziness and lack of discipline, and *no* to others attempting to derail us. No is the most powerful time-and-energy-saving word in the dictionary, but learning to reject people's wishes takes practice. Addiction to the approval of other people is a powerful habit requiring a thoughtful strategy. The desire to be liked has deep roots, and we unconsciously attempt to fulfill this desire even if it's unrealistic and harms us.

For example, I used to give in to unhealthful foods at parties because I didn't want to upset the hostess. I'd eat the cookies, chips, and cake, seeking approval from my friends. I'd also skip workouts when family or friends spontaneously requested my time or help with a chore. I was placing their needs above my own, and it led me to resent them for a favor I chose to do. It isn't logical, it didn't work, and it wasn't in my best interest. When I studied personal development and learned about approval addiction, I realized I was a full-blown addict and started monitoring and altering my behavior. Now I try to say *yes* when I can, but usually say *no* to people and things not in my best interest. This change in behavior has saved me vast amounts of time and energy, and it makes me feel more in control of my life. The only downside is that some people don't understand the concept, and it has cost me a few friends along the way. Take inventory of all the things to which you're saying yes when it comes to eating and exercising, and ask yourself if it's possible to start saying *no*. You don't always have to decline, but even saying no more often will help. It's a habit and worth the price you pay for it.

"Fat people say yes to unhealthful foods and a sedentary lifestyle. Fat losers say no."

Critical Thinking Question

ON A SCALE OF 1-7, 7 AS THE MOST ADDICTED, HOW ADDICTED ARE YOU TO THE APPROVAL OF OTHERS?

Action Step

In the next seven days, say *no* to something that does not serve your best interests and to which you'd normally say *yes*.

MENTAL-TOUGHNESS STRATEGY #7

STOP CARING WHAT FAT PEOPLE THINK

Nearly seventy percent of the U.S. population is overweight or obese. The Center for Disease Control in Atlanta predicts that by 2027, this figure will climb to ninety percent. The obesity epidemic is spinning out of control, and there's no end in sight. Neither the medical community nor the government has the answer. Why listen to people and organizations that are failing to solve the problem? Critical thinking tells us that following failure is illogical and foolish. The masses say diets don't work, yet fit people swear by them. Visit any health club or gym, approach the fittest members, and ask them the role diet plays in their success. They'll all give you the same answer: diet is the most important element. Specifically, diet is eighty percent of the equation and exercise is twenty percent. These numbers are well known in the fitness community, yet fat people continue to reject them.

One of the key lessons in mental-toughness training is breaking emotional addiction to the approval of other people, especially those who are failing. In essence, I'm suggesting that you stop caring what fat people think about diets, exercise, and anything related to fitness. These people may be winners in other areas of life, but in fitness, they're *losing*. You wouldn't take financial advice from a penniless person or medical advice from someone without a medical degree, so why take advice on dieting from fat people? Stop caring and start winning. Losers make excuses. Fat losers achieve results. The one you want to be determines the philosophy you follow.

As obvious as this sounds, most people follow the masses in everything they do, believing strength lies in numbers. The masses are usually wrong, and their ongoing failure to is all the proof you need. Just be aware that if you oppose them, they'll attack and ridicule you. Breaking any addiction you have to their approval is the solution. The bottom line: if you want their results, follow their advice. If you don't, stop caring what they think and start following people who are succeeding. If you want to know where to find them in any town in America, visit your local gym early in the morning or late at night. While fat people are lying on the sofa watching TV and playing video games, the fit people are sculpting their bodies, taking spinning classes, and doing Yoga. Their enthusiasm, discipline, and dedication will inspire you.

"Stop listening to losers. Start listening to fat losers. They're the ones winning the game."

Critical Thinking Question

ON A SCALE OF 1-7, 7 AS THE MOST ADDICTED, HOW ADDICTED ARE YOU TO THE APPROVAL OF OTHER PEOPLE?

Action Step

Take inventory and decide from whom you're taking your dieting and exercise advice.

MENTAL-TOUGHNESS STRATEGY #8

STOP WAITING TO BE RESCUED

As I traveled around the world promoting my best-selling book *Die Fat or Get Tough*, I was astounded at the number of fat people waiting for their government, food manufacturers, pharmaceutical companies, medical experts, and others to save them from themselves. The premise of my book is self-responsibility, and millions of fat people claimed that their condition wasn't their fault. They telephoned by the thousands in Europe every time I was interviewed on the BBC; they scorned me in Australia and threatened to kill me in Manhattan. All because I said if you're fat, it's your fault. After all, whose fault is it?

Stop waiting for the drug company's magic pill. Stop waiting for your doctor to scold you. And stop waiting for Washington to save you. No one is coming to the rescue. You're not a child and it's time to stop eating like one. It's your job to take care of yourself and to stop waiting for Superman to save you. No one can save you, except you. Besides your loved ones, no one cares if you get fit or die fat, and if you become an obesity statistic, you have no one to blame but yourself. And if you're waiting for God to rescue you, stop waiting. Critical thinking demands that you operate from objective reality, and the reality is that no one but you can rescue you from being fat.

"Losers wait to be rescued. Fat losers take control of their eating and exercise habits and become fit. They control their own destinies."

Critical Thinking Question

HAVE YOU BEEN EXPECTING SOMEONE OR SOMETHING TO RESCUE YOU FROM BEING FAT?

Action Step

Decide today that you are the only person who can rescue you from a life of low energy, low self-esteem, and disease. You decide when enough is enough.

MENTAL-TOUGHNESS STRATEGY #9

EAT STRATEGICALLY

I don't know about you, but I was never taught to eat strategically. It turns out, however, that fit people are stoically strategic about the foods they eat, the amount they consume, and the time they eat. Most of the 500 fit people who participated in our two-year study said they ate their biggest meal in the morning and they're smallest one at night. They adhere to a strict regimen of healthful, low-caloric foods in reasonable portions. They are acutely aware of overeating in stressful times and during emotional highs and lows. They consume foods that are easy to digest and produce the energy they need to stay physically active and mentally alert.

These strategies are simple and habitual, and anyone can adopt them. For example, a few years ago I noticed that I tend to overeat when I'm happy and celebrating, so I've identified a more healthful selection of celebratory foods to avoid gaining weight during these times. In the past year, I also stopped eating regular meals at dinner and started drinking healthful and great-tasting protein shakes. I've also cut way back on eating bread, which has made a big difference in my fitness level. These are only a few personal examples of specific strategies created through observation.

You can employ the same strategy for exercise. For example, I've observed that the more consistently I work out, the less I eat and the more motivated I am to stay on my diet. These examples may or may not work for you, but the more aware you become of fit people's habits, as well as your own, the more you'll be able to formulate and customize your personal strategies. Eating strategically makes it easier to become a fat loser.

"Formulate your daily eating strategy with the same intensity you apply to your business or financial strategy and you'll begin seeing almost immediate results."

Critical Thinking Question

ON A SCALE OF 1-7, 7 AS THE BEST, HOW STRATEGIC OF AN EATER ARE YOU?

Action Step

Start implementing strategic eating by deciding which meals will be your largest and smallest. Most expert's recommend making breakfast your largest meal and dinner your smallest.

MENTAL-TOUGHNESS STRATEGY #10

EMBRACE HUNGER

For seven years, our company ran a weight-loss program called *The Fat Losers*, which later morphed into www.fatlosers.com. The single biggest complaint we received was from my suggestion that people embrace hunger and see it as an opportunity to lose weight. I discovered this years ago when I was losing the extra forty pounds I'd gained during a heavy period of traveling around the world delivering speeches. I noticed that every time I went to bed hungry, I weighed less the next morning. I literally became excited about going to bed a little hungry, knowing it was my opportunity to lose weight.

Many people became outraged that I'd suggest you have to go to bed hungry to succeed on a diet. After all, don't those weight-loss diets advertised on TV tell viewers you can eat all you like and still lose weight? They claim that you're never hungry on their diet and the pounds just melt away. If you believe these lies, I have some swampland in Florida I'd like to sell you. The fact is that light hunger, especially at night, is one of the prices you pay to be fit. Unless you're a genetic wonder and can eat everything in sight and never gain weight, you're going to become hungry on your road to becoming a fat loser. This is the place where mental toughness comes into play and gives you the tools to endure long enough to succeed.

"Being hungry before bed tells you you're on the road to losing weight. Embrace the hunger. It is your friend."

Critical Thinking Question

WHEN WAS THE LAST TIME YOU WENT TO BED HUNGRY?

Action Step

Set a goal to go to bed hungry at least three nights during the week and see what happens. Notice that you're hungry when you go to bed but full when you wake up.

MENTAL-TOUGHNESS STRATEGY #11

BEGIN SUFFERING

If some level of physical and emotional suffering weren't required to lose weight, everyone would succeed. Most people fail at every diet they attempt. Weight-loss companies, doctors, and positive-thinking purists love to deny that suffering accompanies any successful diet. In mental-toughness training, we don't deal in positive thinking, political correctness, or self-delusion. We deal in objective reality. In other words, seeing life and the world as it is, not as we wish it were. If you're fat and you want to be fit, you will have to endure some level of suffering, whether you like it or not. That's simply the way it works. Becoming a fat loser is about breaking old habits and implementing new ones, and habit change is difficult to achieve. Just because you decide to stop eating ice cream one day doesn't mean you won't crave it the next. If you're going to succeed, you have to learn to say *no* to yourself and *yes* to more healthful and empowering habits.

According to psychologists, breaking old habits and forming new ones takes twenty-one to thirty days of strict implementation accompanied by mild emotional suffering. After the new habits are formed, only light discipline is required for continued success. So prepare yourself for the suffering process by resolving to stick to your diet and exercise goals, no matter how it makes you feel. When you're tempted to revert to old habitual patterns, remember the amount of pain you've endured from being fat, and imagine the pleasure being fit will bring you. The good news is the suffering is mild, doesn't last long, and will serve as a great source of pride once you arrive at your ideal weight. Suffer the mild pain of habit-change now or suffer the shame, anguish, and self-loathing later. You're already suffering from defeat. Why not suffer your way to victory?

"Fat people suffer more than fat losers. The suffering of victory creates feelings of satisfaction. The suffering of regret only creates additional suffering."

Critical Thinking Question

WOULD YOU RATHER SUFFER THE PAIN OF HABIT-CHANGE AND TEMPORARY-FOOD CRAVINGS OR THE EMOTIONAL REGRET OF ONGOING FAILURE?

Action Step

Make a list of five ways that fat has created emotional suffering in your life, and five ways that becoming a fat loser would enhance your life. Compare the lists and decide whether or not it's worth the effort to suffer your way to success.

MENTAL-TOUGHNESS STRATEGY #12

DETERMINE THE PRICE

Most of the 500 fat people I interviewed failed to invest the time into determining the emotional and physical price they were willing to pay for achieving fitness. As a result of this lack of mental preparation, they quit their diets the first time they experienced pain. The first time I dieted, I did the same thing. I approached it like a hobby and played with it like a toy. When I felt my first craving for sugar, I was shocked and immediately went off the diet. In life, everything has a price. Nothing is free. You either pay the price or you don't. It's that simple. How much of a price are you willing to pay?

I mean, honestly, I like having a muscular physique and I'm willing to pay the price of light daily workouts. But if you told me I had to work out three hours a day to maintain my physique, I'd be unwilling to pay that price. I happily paid $80,000 for my two-door Cadillac, but if you raised the price to $150,000, I wouldn't be willing to invest. Price is relative to how much we want something and how much we think it is worth. When I gained forty pounds, I had to determine the price I was willing to pay to lose it. I'd never gained or lost that much weight before, so I was unsure of the exact price.

I made a list of the amount it was costing me to be fat and the amount I projected it'd cost me to become fit. Like most people, being fat was costing me energy, vitality, confidence, and pride in my appearance. As vain as it sounds, I was used to people telling me how great I looked and I missed the pride and self-confidence that follows the accolades. What it cost to lose the weight was overindulgence, not eating my favorite foods, and having to stave off cravings until my physiology changed. Once I finished this analysis, the price I was willing to pay became clear: I'd do whatever it took to succeed. Twelve weeks later the forty pounds disappeared and my confidence returned. It was worth five times the price I paid. Do your own self-analysis, see if the price matches the benefits, and you'll be more prepared for success.

"Most fat people start their diet without determining the cost and if the benefits are worth the price."

Critical Thinking Question

ON A SCALE OF 1-7, 7 AS ANY PRICE, WHAT PRICE ARE YOU WILLING TO PAY TO BECOME A FAT LOSER?

Action Step

Do a cost-benefit analysis of becoming a fat loser by listing the potential costs and benefits of embarking on a serious journey to fitness.

MENTAL-TOUGHNESS STRATEGY #13

STOP DELUDING YOURSELF

Let's be honest, most of us fall into the psychological trap of self-delusion when it comes to our weight. We walk by the mirror, inhale and maneuver around until we like what we see. For whom are we posturing? It's a mirror. No one is there but a reflection, but the fact is we all do it. I've caught myself doing this over the years and wondering why I'm trying to impress myself with my own physique. It's actually pretty funny when you think about it. Obviously, our self-delusion in this context is designed to reduce the pain of feeling that we're failing in an important area of life, or at least not measuring up to our personal standards. On the surface, this form of self-delusion seems harmless, but it may be the single biggest psychological roadblock we face on our path to becoming a fat loser.

Sucking in your stomach for a photograph, wearing a girdle to hide fat, or donning black to appear thinner are harmless behaviors to fool others, but when the behavior escalates to fooling ourselves, it becomes a problem. Fool the world if you wish, but never fool yourself. Seeing your weight through the eyes of objective reality is the first step to becoming a healthy and fit fat loser. As easy as it is to fall into the self-delusion trap, fat losers avoid it at all costs. Delusion is a disease that creeps up quietly and takes hold when you barely know it's there. Here's an example: If you think you need to lose twenty-five pounds, chances are you need to lose fifty. If you think you need to lose fifty, you probably need to lose a hundred. Never underestimate the power of self-delusion.

One of the strongest underlying forces in the human psyche is the need to feel respected, important, and significant; and being fat makes us feel like losers. That's the reason we delude ourselves. It isn't because we're stupid; on the contrary, we're subconsciously battling for self-preservation. Be sure to do an honest assessment of your current weight. Ask your doctor how much you should lose. Ask him to be completely honest and be mentally tough enough to handle the truth. Then compare your numbers with your doctor's. The difference determines your level of self-delusion.

"Fat people delude themselves into believing they are more fit than they really are. Fat losers see their bodies the same way the world sees them."

Critical Thinking Question

HOW MUCH WEIGHT DO YOU REALLY NEED TO LOSE TO BE AT YOUR BEST?

Action Step

Set a goal in the next seven days to determine an accurate number of pounds you need to lose. Visit your doctor, ask family and friends, and do an objective self-assessment.

MENTAL-TOUGHNESS STRATEGY #14

GROW UP EMOTIONALLY

We all grow up physically. Most people grow up mentally, but only a small percentage of people grow up emotionally. Emotional maturity is rare, and most of us are deluded to the degree in which we possess it. The ultimate example is the psychological leaps of faith people make to believe they will live forever. The prospect of accepting one's own mortality is so emotionally overwhelming to the masses that they will swallow almost anything that refutes reality. The idea that a loved one has died never to be seen again is so horrifying that almost anyone with rhythm in his voice and a microphone in his hand can convince people they will eventually be reunited with their loved ones.

Educated and otherwise sophisticated people can be led like innocent children to believe the unbelievable through blind faith, and it's not because they're stupid. On the contrary, this group includes some extremely bright people. Intelligence and emotional maturity, however, do not always correlate, and this is the place where the breakdown in critical thinking begins.

Becoming a fat loser requires the emotional maturity to accept that you're fat, it's your fault, and you have the emotional strength to change your habits. The first time I appeared on *The Today Show*, Kathie Lee Gifford's co-host, Hoda Kotb, suggested that women couldn't lose weight until they dealt with their underlying

FAT LOSER!

emotional issues. And it's true that a tiny fraction of people need therapy to move forward. There's nothing wrong with finding help if you need it. The fact remains the vast majority of us simply need to grow up emotionally and face the world head-on.

This is the reason why mental toughness is the secret to weight loss. In essence, mental toughness means emotional control, and we all have everything it takes to be emotionally mature and mentally tough. If you don't believe me, listen to a ten-year old cancer patient talk about her disease. These kids have grown mentally strong through the experience of extreme pain and suffering. This extreme discomfort isn't required to become mentally tough, but some catalyst is necessary. The fastest way is to begin to see yourself and the world through the eyes of objective reality. The way you really are as opposed to the way you wish you were. This can be a bitter bill to swallow, but it's the truth. That's the place where mental toughness begins, and emotional maturity is the end result.

"Fat losers approach weight loss like grown-ups. While the masses are acting like children denying their responsibility, fat losers admit their failure and focus on their future success."

Critical Thinking Question

ON A SCALE OF 1-7, 7 AS THE MOST MATURE, HOW EMOTIONALLY MATURE ARE YOU? DETERMINE YOUR SCORE BY HOW OBJECTIVELY YOU VIEW YOURSELF AND THE WORLD.

Action Step

Make a decision to take one hundred percent of the responsibility for becoming fat. It's not partly your fault; it's every bit your fault. Accept responsibility and move on.

MENTAL-TOUGHNESS STRATEGY #15

REMEMBER FAT SICKENS AND KILLS

Being fat is a dangerous condition leading to heart disease, cancer, diabetes, sexual dysfunction, high blood pressure, and a host of other debilitating, deadly diseases, not to mention low energy, decreased vitality, and mental sluggishness. In other words, being fat is all bad. There are no redeeming qualities. Seventy percent of the U.S. population is gambling with their lives, yet many of them are unaware of it. In the age of political correctness, people who care about us won't tell us we're fat. Instead, they enable us by saying we are big-boned, plus-sized, or pleasingly plump.

When beloved actor James Gandolfini died of a heart attack in 2013, the autopsy stated he died of "natural" causes. A fifty-one-year-old man dies of a heart attack and they call it "natural causes." Any competent physician will tell you a fifty-one-year-old man shouldn't be keeling over with a heart attack. James Gandolfini was six feet tall and weighed almost 300 pounds. The man was morbidly obese. His untimely death is a cautionary tale, but the mainstream press focused on his acting contributions and how sad it was that he died so young, leaving behind a young son and a wonderful family. The press missed a great opportunity to use his story as a warning to people whistling passed the graveyard with their weight.

I have a friend who is sixty-one, five-feet, ten-inches and weighs 350 pounds. He's been toying with diet and exercise for twenty years. Even though he's suffered serious health consequences from being obese, he's never taken dieting seriously. I saw him a few weeks ago and he said, "Steve, I just can't stick to a diet. I know it's killing me, but I just can't do it." I told him there's no way he believes his weight is going to kill him. If he did, he'd lose the weight. He laughed it off, but he is James Gandolfini waiting to happen. The bottom line is becoming a fat loser and getting fit is not a game. Your life is on the line. Just because you think rattlesnakes are cute doesn't mean they won't kill you. Next time you're tempted to cheat on your diet, remember, your health is serious business, and failure is not an option.

"Fat people are heart attacks waiting to happen; they're digging their own graves with a knife and fork."

Critical Thinking Question

ON A SCALE OF 1-7, 7 AS THE MOST DANGEROUS, HOW MUCH PHYSICAL DANGER IS EXCESSIVE FAT CAUSING YOU?

Action Step

Set a goal to move out and stay out of the obesity danger zone.

MENTAL-TOUGHNESS STRATEGY #16

STOP LETTING YOURSELF OFF THE HOOK

If you had a child who continually played in highway traffic, risking his life by dodging cars, would you slap him on the wrist when he ignored you about staying off the highway? I don't think so. As a matter of fact, you'd probably scold him within an inch of his life and ground him for a month. After all, his very life would be at risk. Being fat is no different except it's a discrete, quiet killer that sneaks up on you a little more every year before it snuffs out your life. We've all been on diets at one time or another and most of us have failed to stay on them. I'm not suggesting you beat yourself up for failing. Berating yourself won't help. I'm suggesting you make a decision to stop letting yourself off the hook for cheating on or abandoning your diet. Stop starting over and telling yourself you'll do it next time. There is no next time, only this time right now. You said next time, last time, and allowing yourself the luxury of continually quitting is a deadly habit.

Forget about yesterday, last week, or last year. The past is over. Focus all of your mental energy on the present and micro-manage your diet down to one meal at a time until you build the confidence to know you're strong enough to stay on it. If you keep letting yourself off the hook by succumbing to cravings, peer pressure, emotional swings, and other distractions, you'll continue to run in circles until you eventually drop dead. Forget about tomorrow because it's a promissory note. You only have today, one meal at a time. Everything else is past or future and out of your control, so why waste time and energy worrying about it? Hold your own feet to the fire, stay on the diet, and break the cycle of dieting failure once and for all. You'll be glad you did.

"Stop starting over on Monday.

Monday is never coming."

Critical Thinking Question

ON A SCALE OF 1-7, 7 AS THE MOST COMMITTED, HOW COMMITTED ARE YOU TO ACHIEVING YOUR IDEAL WEIGHT ON THIS DIET?

Action Step

Decide to do "whatever it takes" to become fit this time around. Create a massive reward for yourself when you reach your ideal weight and tell everyone you know about your goal in order to create additional pressure.

MENTAL-TOUGHNESS STRATEGY #17

STOP MAKING EXCUSES

There's no excuse for being fat. It's a combination of laziness, failure to prepare, lack of exercise, poor food choices, emotional eating, and a host of other self-induced habitual behaviors. I should know because I've fallen into every one of these traps myself. I'm not throwing rocks from an ivory tower. If I told you that you had one year to become fit or you'd be executed, I promise you in twelve months you'd look fantastic. Do genetics play a role in the difficulty of losing weight? Yes. Do many women have a tougher time losing weight than men? Sure. Do some people have underlying emotional issues creating additional obstacles to becoming fit? Of course. The bottom line is that no matter how easy or difficult it is for any of us to lose weight, it can be done. If you decide to become a fat loser and stay on your diet, you'll succeed, whether you believe it or not.

Only two requirements are necessary to becoming a fat loser: first, find a healthful and effective diet. Second, have the mental toughness to stay on it until you reach your goal weight. And that's it, nothing more and nothing less. All the excuses we hear on TV about addictive foods, cortisol (hydrocortisone), the evil food manufactures, and all the other excuses are irrelevant. While these things are interesting, they are not important. Selecting a good diet is easy. If you need help, ask your doctor. After that, your success boils down to one: are you mentally tough enough to stay on the diet? There is no in-between. You either are or you are not. The scale will tell the story. Don't waste your time making excuses because none are available. So you're fat, so what? So are 1.4 billion other people in the world. Now it's time to resolve the issue. Grow up emotionally, toughen up, and solve the problem.

"Excuses are for losers. If you want to become a fat loser, it's time to let them go."

Critical Thinking Question

HOW MUCH HAS MAKING EXCUSES COST YOU IN MONEY, RELATIONSHIPS, HEALTH, AND OTHER IMPORTANT AREAS OF LIFE?

Action Step

Make a list of all the excuses you've used in the past for failing on a diet and decide to eliminate all of them this time around.

MENTAL-TOUGHNESS STRATEGY #18

WORK HARDER ON YOU THAN ON YOUR DIET

Most people lose weight and regain it because they failed to address their underlying issues behind growing fat in the first place. After interviewing 500 fat and 500 fit people, I discovered some of the psychological challenges leading people to become yo-yo dieters. For instance, some women stay fat to thwart unwanted attention from men after a traumatic experience of sexual abuse. Others use food to medicate themselves for a variety of reasons in the same way alcoholics and drug addicts do. People like me become busy and stop paying attention to what they're eating and wake up one day forty pounds overweight.

There are dozens of reasons for becoming fat, and simply losing weight won't resolve the issue. Becoming a fat loser solves the problem of effect but not the cause. Only personal development can assure that solution. The self-help industry is a fifteen-billion-dollar-a-year business in the United States for a reason; it works. The masses scoff and scorn people who study personal growth. They say it's for simpletons, calling its practitioners mere purveyors of the obvious and castigate its students for being naïve. While the critics are crowing, personal-development fans are growing smarter, savvier, richer, and more fit every day. One group spends its life watching people live their dreams while the other makes them reality. Whatever caused you to become fat can be overcome by analyzing your belief system around food, dieting, and exercise. The key is raising your level of consciousness in these areas. Read personal-development books, attend seminars, and watch YouTube videos by thought leaders. Be willing to invest in yourself and you'll become more self-aware. Most people graduate from high school or college and never read a book again, at least not books about improvement. Most people never invest money and time in attending a seminar across the country. Then again, most people die fat, penniless, and unfulfilled.

According to Gallup, the number-one deathbed regret people have is, "I wish I'd have lived life on my own terms and taken more chances." You don't need to fall into this trap. The world of self-improvement is available and waiting. It changed my life and it can change yours.

Albert Einstein once said, "A problem cannot be solved at the same level of thinking that created it." The thinking that made you fat won't make you thin. Embrace personal development and elevate your consciousness to a level at which being fat is unacceptable.

Critical Thinking Question

HAVE YOU ADDRESSED AND DEALT WITH THE UNDERLYING CAUSES THAT MADE YOU FAT?

Action Step

Read *177 Mental Toughness Secrets of the World Class*. This book will help you make the distinction between middle- and world-class thinking.
www.mentaltoughnesssecrets.com

MENTAL-TOUGHNESS STRATEGY #19

STOP STARTING OVER

How many of us have started diets only to abandon them midway to our goal weight? I know I have and I'll bet you have, too. Start-Stop syndrome is a common cause of weight-loss failure. The root cause of this success-killing disease is the belief that time is unlimited, and another opportunity will be available to become fit. Tell the millions of Americans who have heart attacks, cancer, and diabetes caused by obesity. One of the core philosophies of fat-losers states: "There is no tomorrow." Yesterday's gone and tomorrow is never guaranteed. Today is all you have and now is the time to succeed. Forget about all the times you started over. It doesn't matter anymore. It's in the rearview mirror, never to be heard from or seen again. Living in the now is the way of the fat loser because the present is the only time you can make a difference.

The next time you slip off your diet, don't turn it into a disaster by saying, "I've already cheated, and I might as well keep eating and begin again on Monday." This excuse is easy to use and I've used it myself. It's a mind-trap designed to relieve the psychological and physiological pressure that early-stage dieting can cause, and it's cognitive quicksand. No end is possible with the start-stop syndrome. Once it becomes a habit, it becomes easier and easier

STEVE SIEBOLD 63

to quit. The next time you're tempted to fall into this insidious mental sinkhole, say to yourself with authority, "There is no tomorrow." This kind of psychological programming builds mental toughness and keeps you on the path to fat-loser success.

> *"Starting over is for losers. Fat losers know there is no tomorrow."*

Critical Thinking Question

WHAT REWARD WOULD YOU HAVE TO PROMISE YOURSELF TO REFRAIN FROM RESTARTING YOUR DIET?

Action Step

Make a decision to pay the price of becoming a fat loser, without having to start over. Why continue paying half the price and repeatedly suffering through early stages of dieting?

STEVE SIEBOLD

MENTAL-TOUGHNESS STRATEGY #20

BEGIN STARING

We're taught as children it's impolite to stare. Mom was right, but I suggest you begin staring for a specific reason and only at a particular group. Most fit people are not genetic wonders like many of the movie stars in Hollywood. The first time I attended the Academy Awards in 2013, I had an opportunity to spend time with screen-siren Halle Berry. As we were posing for a photograph, I placed my arm around Halle's waist and it practically wrapped all the way around her. Jennifer Aniston is the same way, as are many of the sexy movie stars we admire. But the fact is these women are genetic wonders. They were born with goddess-shaped figures and racehorse metabolisms. The rest of us have to work much harder to sculpt our physique and maintain our diets. It requires discipline, dedication, and persistence in a world of culinary temptations. That's the reason why staring at and admiring fat losers is a great habit.

Don't merely stare, compliment them on their success and ask them for their secret. Everyone who has paid the price for success loves to be recognized, and his or her response will inspire you to stay on track. Staring at them will help you build a fat-loser consciousness whereby all you seem to notice are the people winning the fitness game. Form this habit by joining a health club and notice all the muscled bodies. Most of the people you'll see working out will be fat losers. Fat people rarely join health clubs, which is one of the reasons they're fat. So join a club, start exercising every day, and stare at all the beautiful bodies in the building. It is enjoyable as well as inspiring, and it will program your mind for success.

"Stop glaring at fat people in the buffet line, and begin staring at the beach bodies you want to emulate."

Critical Thinking Question

HAVE YOU DETERMINED THE KIND OF BODY FOR WHICH YOU'RE STRIVING?

Action Step

Create a vision board by pasting pictures of bodies you want to emulate on a poster board and put it in a place you frequent every day.

MENTAL-TOUGHNESS STRATEGY #21

STOP LISTENING TO DOCTORS

When I interviewed doctors for my book *Die Fat or Get Tough*, I was shocked to discover how reluctant most of them were to tell their patients the truth about their weight. They repeatedly told me they were afraid of losing patients. Isn't this their job? Yes and no. *Yes*, ideally, your doctor should be tough enough to tell you the truth and successful enough to risk losing a patient. However, in the age of political correctness, many physicians are terrified of offending fat patients and feeling their wrath financially.

The majority of doctors I interviewed cited the emotional immaturity and psychological vulnerability of their patients as the primary reason for their silence. Dr. Alok Trivedi addressed this matter in his controversial book *Why Doctors Lie about Weight Loss*. According to Dr. Trivedi, doctors say many patients don't take responsibility for their health, so why should the doctor put his or her neck on the line? He also says that many patients think they know more about their weight issues than their doctors. The days of trusting your doctor with your life are over. Marcus Welby is dead.*

A friend of mine is a twenty-nine-year-old woman who stands five-feet, four-inches and weighs 250 pounds. Her doctor recently told her she was healthy. When she told me this news I said, "Healthy compared to whom, James Gandolfini?" She was not amused. This is an example of the medical community's unwillingness to take a stand and help patients become fit.

In 2013, the American Medical Association met in Chicago and declared that obesity is a disease. This statement was the most irresponsible decision they've made to date. It will discourage millions of fat people who believe they have a disease that they are powerless to overcome. They will simply stop trying. This decision was a money move, pure and simple, with no regard for the fat people it will disempower. Now doctors can bill insurance companies for telling patients they have *obesity disease.* As ludicrous as this term sounds, the AMA is using it with impunity. Don't believe it for a second. If you're fat, you eat too much and exercise too little. Cancer is a disease. Obesity is a self-induced condition. And there's a world of difference between the two. The next time you visit your doctor, buyer beware.

"Doctors in America are practicing medicine in a state of fear. Frightened people tell half-truths."

---

*A reference to the 1970s fictional television doctor, Marcus Welby, MD.

Critical Thinking Question

WHO IS IN CHARGE OF YOUR HEALTHCARE, YOU OR YOUR DOCTOR?

Action Step

Read *Why Doctors Lie about Weight Loss* by Dr. Alok Trivedi.

MENTAL-TOUGHNESS STRATEGY #22

STOP MAKING WEIGHT LOSS COMPLEX

Let's be honest, losing weight is simple. It may not be easy, but it is simple. It's only a two-step process. Step One: select a good diet. Step Two: develop the mental toughness to follow it. There is nothing else. That's the reason health clubs across America are overflowing with fat losers who decided to become fit. Staying on a diet isn't always easy, especially in the beginning, but the simplicity of the process cannot be denied. This process is common sense, but I've debated dozens of doctors in the media who insist that losing weight is far more complex. They cite the common obstacles: cortisol, addictive food ingredients, oversized portions, emotional issues, genetic factors, and so on. By their assessment, it's a miracle any of us ever escape the confines of obesity. While all of these factors are legitimate obstacles requiring increased mental toughness, there's nothing complex about them.

If you notice that some foods are addictive, avoid them. If you have emotional issues you can't resolve, seek therapy. If you're served large-portion sizes, only eat half. This is adolescent logic doctors don't believe we're capable of following, which I find insulting. Some doctors would like you to believe you can't become a fat loser without them. At best, it's an ego-power play. At worst, it's mass manipulation designed to keep you worshiping at their altar. Mental toughness calls for independent thinking and self-assessment, which is the opposite of mass consciousness. The secret to becoming a fat loser is being mentally strong enough to stay on your diet when you're hungry or when you experience an emotional trigger. It's that simple, and it becomes easier every day you do it.

"Economics is complicated. Quantum theory is complicated. Losing weight is not complicated."

Critical Thinking Question

ARE YOU MENTALLY TOUGH ENOUGH TO STAY ON YOUR DIET LONG ENOUGH TO BECOME A FAT LOSER?

Action Step

Give yourself the ultimate test to see if you are naturally mentally tough: if your children were trapped inside your house as it was burning to the ground and the fire department refused to enter, would you sit on the side and wait for your family to die or would you try to save them, knowing the odds were stacked against you?

Now tell me you don't have the mental strength to lose weight.

MENTAL-TOUGHNESS STRATEGY #23

START PRIORITIZING EXERCISE

During my interviews with fat and fit people, I was stunned to discover the differences in thinking the two groups had regarding exercise. The fat people saw exercise as a chore they didn't have time to pursue, while the fit people believed exercise was a critical part of their daily routine. Some of them even called exercise "a privilege." Regular exercise has so many benefits it's almost impossible to overstate them. And I'm not talking about becoming a gym rat or working out two hours a day. I'm simply suggesting low-impact, moderate exercise such as walking, swimming, weight training, and others in that category.

Remember, we're not trying to turn you into a body builder or fitness model; we're only trying to make you a fat loser instead of just fat. Becoming a fat loser doesn't require extreme exercise or a hard-core regimen. Those are for people who are already fat losers and want to move to the next level. Let's help you to become fit before we start training you for the Marines. While staying on your diet will represent about eighty percent of your success, the other twenty percent will be consistent, light-scale exercise. If you can build the habit of exercising five days a week for thirty to forty-five minutes a day, that's all you'll need for the exercise portion of becoming a fat loser. Diet will do the rest. The key is making exercise a priority instead of a luxury. The psychological momentum you'll experience through regular exercise will be substantial, and it will directly affect your diet. When you're exercising regularly, you become more sensitive about food selections, gain more confidence, and experience fewer emotional mood swings. Exercise is loaded with benefits, so discover them by starting today.

"In the world of fat losers, dieting is king and exercise is queen. You need both to succeed."

Critical Thinking Question

WHAT DO YOU BELIEVE ABOUT EXERCISE THAT'S KEPT YOU FROM ENGAGING IN IT?

Action Step

Do whatever it takes to carve out thirty to forty-five minutes of your daily schedule to exercise.

MENTAL-TOUGHNESS STRATEGY #24

SHORE UP YOUR BALANCE SHEET

If you want to see the way you became fat, break down the food you eat into accounting terms. The healthful, lean, nutritious foods are listed as assets and the unhealthful foods as liabilities. Once you put them on a balance sheet, it's easy to see the way you grew fat. I tried this method back in 2001 when I had gained forty pounds. I started writing down all the foods I ate following this format, and the bottom line wasn't pretty. I had accrued ninety percent liabilities and ten percent assets. Today my balance sheet looks much better, as does my waistline.

A company with mostly liabilities and few assets is difficult to operate, and cannot remain in business. Your body is the most important entity you'll ever own. The question is are you building its assets? Any accountant will tell you that reducing liabilities is a good idea. The doughnuts, pizza, bagels, chips, hamburgers, and cookies are all liabilities. They drag us down, give us heartburn, deplete our energy, and make us fat. On the other side of the ledger, foods such as fish, lean meats, vegetables, fruits, and other natural and nutritious foods, are assets. They deliver energy, vitality, mental clarity, focus, and make us feel good inside and out. These foods make us fat losers. Increasing assets while reducing debt is the goal, and debt is more than just a simple liability. It is dangerous because as the interest accrues, (as time goes on) it systematically robs us of good health.

Debt is the heart attack waiting to happen, or the cancer or diabetes waiting to be diagnosed. When we're eating unhealthful foods, our debt is accruing quietly and slowly, and we barely notice it. Then one day we wake up and the payment is due. Did James Gandolfini wake up one day and suddenly have a massive heart attack? No, the problem had been growing in his body for years. The day of his heart attack was the day his debt was due.

Begin writing down everything you eat and balance your ledger at the end of the day. Be sure to include physical exercise as an asset. This Mental-Toughness Strategy allows you to see eating and exercise habits in a whole new light, paving the way to greater clarity.

"Operate your body like a business and you will become an unstoppable fat loser."

Critical Thinking Question

IF YOUR FOOD SELECTIONS WERE ACTUALLY BUSINESS ASSETS AND LIABILITIES, WOULD YOU STILL BE IN BUSINESS?

Action Step

Just for today, divide your food selections into assets and liabilities to see where you stand.

MENTAL-TOUGHNESS STRATEGY #25

STOP WHINING AND START SUCCEEDING

Most of us fail at dieting, myself included, until we become serious about it. Dieting is a linear process. In other words, if you stay on it, you *will* lose weight. There's no mystery in it. You can kick, scream, complain, moan, or stomp your feet, but as long as you remain one hundred percent compliant, you'll succeed. The only way to fail is treating your diet like a plaything, changing it to meet your cravings and thinking you're going to beat the system. I repeat, if you've tried this tactic, don't slash your wrists or jump off of a bridge. You're in the majority. Most of us have fallen into these traps. The key is to stop whining and start winning. I'm not talking about getting into body-building-bikini shape. I'm talking about saving your life by committing to diet and exercise. If you want to lose ten to fifteen pounds and build a beach body, go for it. There's nothing that strokes the ego better than walking down a beach with people staring at your muscled body. It makes you feel like a million bucks. But whether your goal is losing a hundred pounds and saving your life or building a world-class physique, the strategy is the same. Stop failing at dieting and begin fulfilling your desires. That means being as committed to your diet as you are to your kids, your spouse, or other important people in your life.

Dieting is a zero-sum game, an all-or-nothing proposition that requires complete adherence to the goal. You have to execute the process with one hundred percent integrity, completing every facet of the process you promised yourself. People fail because they're ninety percent committed and the remaining ten percent is the part in which the weight is lost. It's like pumping iron: those last two reps you can barely manage are the ones that build the muscle. All the reps before that were simply preparing the muscle to be stressed enough for growth to occur. And yes, most people omit the last two reps and miss the benefit. The secret is deciding to interrupt and end the cycle of stopping short. It's not difficult, but it is a drastic change in habit for most of us. The good news is it's worth it. Being a fat loser is much more enjoyable than being fat, and the more you lose, the more enjoyment you will experience.

"Failing at dieting costs more emotionally than succeeding. Decide to suffer once and reap the rewards forever."

Critical Thinking Question

HOW MANY MORE TIMES WILL YOU PUT A MEDIOCRE EFFORT INTO YOUR DIET BEFORE YOU REALIZE SUCCESS IS NON-NEGOTIABLE?

Action Step

Make a list of all the excuses you've made over the years for failing on diets, and ask this: why will this time be different?

MENTAL-TOUGHNESS STRATEGY #26

EMBRACE EMOTIONAL SUPPORT

My dad was a tough guy. His dad was even tougher, so I grew up thinking emotional support was for sissies. Then one day life became rough and this hard core philosophy wasn't enough. I reluctantly reached out for support and my mom, dad and wife were there to provide it. It was a wonderful lesson I'll never forget. Going it alone works at times, but when you're really feeling the heat, it's comforting to have caring people in your corner. The obvious times to seek support are those when you lose a loved one, get a divorce, lose a job, or some other equally upsetting situation. We all know about calling on our support team during *those* times, so why wouldn't we call on them when we're dieting? Why do so many of us attempt to fight the goliath that has slain us so many times and think we have a serious chance of winning on our own? Becoming a fat loser is certainly a simple process, but it's not easy breaking thirty or forty years of eating habits ingrained in your consciousness like the multiplications tables you learned in grammar school. These habits are like steel cables that are difficult to sever.

Dieting is a dogfight, and calling in support from friends and family is an intelligent strategy. Studies indicate overwhelmingly that people with strong support systems have a much higher success rate in the weight-loss process than people who don't. This means sitting down or calling the person and telling him or her about the journey on which you're about to embark and asking for support along the way. Explain that while you're fully committed to a successful outcome on a specific date, experience has shown that you may have moments of weakness, personal or professional challenges, or everyday events that threaten to derail your success, and you'd like to know you can call if you need support. Many people make the mistake of assuming a friend or family member will automatically lend support, only to arrive at a weak moment and discover that person didn't know you were dieting. People only know what you tell them, and if you were planning to sail around the world, start a business, or marry, you'd surely let them know. Becoming a fat loser is an important goal since it may save your life or make it better. The bottom line is that dieting is a big deal and gaining emotional support serves as an insurance policy for your success.

"Fat people think they have to fight the battle of the bulge alone. Fat losers build a support team to help them navigate through the storms everyone faces along the way."

Critical Thinking Question

HOW MANY PEOPLE WOULD YOU HAVE ON YOUR IDEAL SUPPORT TEAM?

Action Step

Make a list of all the people you want on your support team and begin calling them one by one and asking for their help.

FAT LOSER!

MENTAL-TOUGHNESS STRATEGY #27

ACCEPT REALITY

The power of psychological delusion in the weight-loss process is formidable. Looking in the mirror and seeing the image you want to see instead of your real self creates a disassociation between fantasy and reality. Again, this is another trap into which I fell when I was overweight. It took going to a friend's wedding and being embarrassed that people were struggling to recognize me to wake me up to objective reality. Accepting reality also applies to analyzing your eating habits from an outsider's point of view. Fat people don't become overweight because they have healthful eating habits; they become overweight because they eat like *fat* people. Have you ever noticed that the buffet-style restaurants are overflowing with fat people? We have a popular buffet restaurant near our summer home in Georgia and our winter home in Florida, and at least ninety percent of the people I see in these places are overweight, with about sixty percent obese. Why are these people in buffet-style restaurants? For the same reason drunks go to bars: *they're in denial*.

People don't purposely eat or drink themselves to death. It's a long, drawn-out method of suicide. The truth is that drunks and morbidly obese people share the same fantasy of being in control of their unpleasant habits. If this person is you, here's your wake-up call: accept reality. If you were in control, *you wouldn't be fat*. Your eating habits are slowly killing you and you're allowing it to happen. Stop being stupid and start thinking like the educated person you are. All drunks think they can have one more drink and every loser in Vegas thinks they're going to hit the jackpot. The reality is you can't solve this problem until you realize you have one.

It's easy to avoid reality because it can be harsh and even cruel, but that doesn't change the fact that *it's real*. I've been criticized around the world for calling people fat instead of large, pleasingly plump, or big boned. The fact is none of these labels are accurate, and more important they soften the harsh reality of failure that enables and empowers people to continue to fail. I don't call people fat to be mean. I call people fat because I care about them and believe in their capacity to handle the truth and change their ways. Calling someone *ugly* is mean. Calling someone overweight is a gift of love, because fat can be altered. After shunning the supernatural in my book *Sex, Politics, Religion: How Delusional Thinking is Destroying America*, reporters and people worldwide have questioned me about my beliefs. I believe in humanity. I believe we all have the power and capacity to accept the harsh facts of life and thrive within the confines of objective reality. A life clouded with whimsical fantasy is a wasted life. Being fat is reality for some of us, and being fit is reality for others. It all boils down to the way you want to spend your life. Do you want to live in the real world or fantasyland? Many fat people choose fantasyland, which is the reason why America is headed to a ninety percent overweight population. It's time for you to choose. I hope you'll decide to accept reality and face it without reservation or fear.

> *"Fat people pretend they aren't overweight and that being fat doesn't matter. Fat losers wake up, embrace reality, and get fit."*

Critical Thinking Question

WHEN IT COMES TO YOUR WEIGHT, ARE YOU "WHISTLING PAST THE GRAVEYARD"?

Action Step

Decide to wake up and see the world as it is, and yourself as you actually are, instead of mentally medicating yourself with childish fantasy.

MENTAL-TOUGHNESS STRATEGY #28

STOP BEHAVING LIKE A CHILD

Children are wonderful. They're enjoyable, creative, imaginative, and energetic. They believe they can be, do, and have anything because the world hasn't negatively programmed them yet. The brainwashing takes time, and it's beautiful to watch a free and fearless mind approach every aspect of life as if it's mystery and a miracle. That's the upside of a child's mentality. The downside is children are emotionally immature. Examples include not doing what they say they will do, lying to themselves and others, and quitting as soon as instant gratification fades away. We don't become too upset when kids do these things because, after all, they're only children.

The problem arises when many of them evolve physically and mentally but fail to mature emotionally. Physical and mental maturation occurs naturally whereas emotional maturity combines natural evolution with conscious decision-making. In other words, consciously or unconsciously, part of our emotional maturation is a personal decision. For example, let's say someone cuts you off in traffic. This frightens you at first, but your fear then turns to anger. Seeking immediate gratification through revenge, the childish response would be to scream at the driver in the car that cut you off. We've all done this and know it's a silly, futile, and potentially dangerous response. The mature driver refuses to seek revenge and calmly moves down the highway removing the threat of any further danger. This action is emotional maturity.

Dieting is no different. When we say we're going to lose weight but don't, lie about it to others, and quit when we don't see instant results, we are, in essence, behaving like children. When it comes to becoming fit, there's no room for childlike thinking. You're not playing flashlight tag or a video game; you're fighting for your life. Dieting is serious business and emotional maturity is required. Becoming a fat loser means growing up emotionally, becoming mentally tough and succeeding. So decide today that enough is enough and it's time to do the work you've been promising yourself for years. That's the way rational-thinking adults operate. Establish a goal, remain strong, and ultimately win.

"Become a fat loser by thinking like an adult.

Children break promises. Mature adults do not."

Critical Thinking Question

ARE YOU EMOTIONALLY PREPARED TO ABANDON ALL EXCUSES AND LOSE THE WEIGHT ONCE AND FOR ALL?

Action Step

Rate yourself on an emotional maturity scale of 1-7, 7 as the most mature. If you score less than a five, you'll remain fat until you mature.

MENTAL-TOUGHNESS STRATEGY #29

BEGIN COMPARTMEN-TALIZING

Mental toughness equates to emotional control, and dieting for most of us is highly emotional. It's critical to have the ability to control, manipulate, and compartmentalize your emotions. Emotional Compartmentalization (EC) is the ability to concentrate fully on a task without becoming distracted by external or internal forces.

EC is a learned psychological skill that allows you to avoid becoming emotionally overwhelmed with problems, challenges, struggles, and threats that dominate your thoughts, thus distracting you from focusing on the task at hand. An example is Tiger Woods, who is highly trained and skilled in EC. He has earned millions on the golf course, blocking out distractions with which other golfers struggle.

Woods was a master at EC until his personal life began to unravel, his wife left him, and worldwide media made him a whipping boy for marital infidelity. Suddenly, Tiger had a hitch in his swing, a hesitation in his step, and the critics crowed about the end of his reign. His world ranking plummeted from #1 to #58 and the buzzards began to circle. Other golfers began believing that Tiger was not only human, but also *beatable*. Even some of the biggest names in golf were eulogizing the late, great Tiger. That's when the golf channel called and asked me to appear and discuss Tiger's

STEVE SIEBOLD 93

toughness. I agreed and professed to millions of golfers that Tiger was *still* Tiger, but he was experiencing emotional overload on a global scale. I told them once he worked through it, he'd come rocketing back better than ever. I made this statement in every major golf magazine, and a great many people laughed. Of course the rest is history. Within a few years, Tiger Woods came roaring back with a vengeance and reclaimed his #1 ranking. This forecast was an easy prediction because this performer was trained to block out any distraction threatening his performance.

EC in dieting may not be as dramatic as concentration for Tiger Woods, but it has the power to shield you in the same way. Let's take holidays, for instance. You're on your diet and doing great, and now you're at a Christmas party flooded with cookies, candy, and cake. The hostess seems offended by guests not gorging on her food, and now you have to use EC to block out the food and the hostess. It's not easy, but it is simple. You only have to decide the most important element in this equation. The answer is you and your diet, so walk away from the fatty foods because they aren't your friends. Graciously explain your dieting situation to the hostess and ask for her support. If she gives it to you, you're all set. If she doesn't, leave the party immediately.

Dieting is not a game. Heavy drinkers seeking sobriety don't socialize with drunks at bars, and if they happen to find themselves in that situation, they quickly leave. EC requires the emotional maturity to say no to situations and people not aligned with your goal. All obstacles must be overcome or removed. You can practice EC in every area of your life by timing how long you can focus on one task at a time to the exclusion of all else. Eventually you'll become a master of this critical skill.

"The ability to direct one hundred percent of your mental energy toward a selected target for an extended time is attainable for anyone through practice."

Critical Thinking Question

ON A SCALE OF 1-7, 7 AS THE BEST, HOW EFFECTIVE ARE YOU IN EMOTIONAL COMPARTMENTALIZATION?

Action Step

Start practicing EC during every important task, and see how long you can concentrate on it before your focus is redirected.

MENTAL-TOUGHNESS STRATEGY #30

STOP ACTING FAT

In the 1970s, I played on the national junior tennis circuit. In the 1980s, I played college and professional tennis. I could run a mile in less than five minutes and play competitive tennis for four hours at full strength. Despite my physical prowess, however, I behaved like a fat person in many ways. For instance, I ate junk food my entire career. I stayed up late and didn't sleep enough. I didn't eat a nutritious diet because I didn't believe I needed one. Once I retired, became older, and went into business, I did something else fat people do: I stopped paying attention to my eating and exercise habits. All this fat-thinking eventually resulted in a forty-pound weight gain. First, I had to stop thinking and acting like a fat person, and within a few months, I became a fat loser.

If you're going to succeed, you have to start acting like a fit person by finding and staying on a healthful diet. That means making exercise a priority in your life and treating it with the same importance as brushing your teeth or taking a shower. It also means never resting on your laurels, believing you've arrived. Remember, the human psyche is a delicate, intricate, and complex mechanism. One idiosyncrasy is that it never remains stagnant. It's either growing or it's dying, advancing or retreating, moving forward or backward. There is no stagnation when it comes to consciousness. You're either expanding or contracting. That's the reason dieting is a lifelong process, so you continue to advance, move forward, and expand rather than the opposite. Consciousness stagnation is not an option. It doesn't exist. Focus on thinking and acting like a fit person, not a fat one. Fat-person thinking won't make you thinner any more than middle-class thinking will make you richer. Your success begins with your mindset; the rest is the biochemical diet you follow. If you want to learn more about the way fit people think, join a health club and ask members about their beliefs around food, exercise, diet, and discipline. Their being-fit mentality is the foundation of their success.

"Fat thinkers act fat. Fat losers act fit even when they're fat."

Critical Thinking Question

REGARDLESS OF YOUR CURRENT WEIGHT, DO YOU THINK LIKE A FAT OR FIT PERSON?

Action Step

Make a list of the fat and fit beliefs and philosophies you follow and see if they are congruent with your results.

MENTAL-TOUGHNESS STRATEGY #31

STOP SOCIALIZING WITH FAT PEOPLE

When I was competing on the national junior tennis circuit in the 1970s, I met many rich kids. Our family was upper-middle class, but some of the families of the kids with whom I trained and competed against were just plain wealthy. Some were even what you might call "hog-nasty rich." I never gave it much thought in the beginning, until the summer of 1977 when my doubles partner invited me to stay at his family's home in an upscale suburb of Chicago. He said we could practice all weekend at his house because he had a tennis court in his backyard. I'd seen backyard courts on TV, but never in real life, and I certainly never met anyone who had one. Needless to say, I jumped at the chance and spent the weekend practicing on this beautifully manicured tennis court behind this palatial estate.

That weekend I decided I wanted to be rich. I shared this thought with my friends, but they laughed and told me rich people were mobsters, crooks, or just plain evil. But I couldn't forget the image of the backyard tennis court, so in 1984, my sophomore year in college, I started interviewing millionaires. This project turned into an obsession that continues to this day. I've now interviewed more than 1,200 millionaires and billionaires, and my case study has been cited worldwide, culminating in the publication of my best-selling book, *How Rich People Think*. The idea that *thinking* was the secret of their success was the greatest lesson the wealthy have taught me over the past thirty years. Rich people think differently about money than do the poor or middle classes, and these differences in thinking are the reasons for their wealth. Their advice to associate with rich people and limit my exposure to the consciousness of financially struggling people made me a millionaire.

The same principle applies to fit people. If you want to be fit, spend more time around fit people. Listen to the way they talk about diet, exercise, and everything related to fitness. Their thinking on this subject is the root cause of their success. Limit your exposure to fat people. The more you listen to them whine and complain about the difficulties of dieting and working out, the more you'll descend to their level of thinking. As Albert Einstein said, "Consciousness is contagious." I'm not suggesting that fit people are better than fat people, or that rich people are better than poor people. But when it comes to achieving results, socialize with winners in the areas of life in which you want to win. The exposure to the winner's consciousness is worth its weight in gold.

"If you want healthful, loving relationships, socialize with people having healthful, loving relationships. If you want to be rich, socialize with rich people. If you want to be fit, socialize with fit people. Mom was right: we become like the people we hang around most."

Critical Thinking Question

HOW FIT ARE THE PEOPLE WITH WHOM YOU SOCIALIZE MOST?

Action Step

Start spending more time with fit people and ask them about the way they became fit and how they are able to maintain it.

MENTAL-TOUGHNESS STRATEGY #32

BEGIN KEEPING YOUR WORD

The concept of personal integrity rarely arises when people talk about diets. You hear the words willpower, discipline, self-denial, delayed gratification, and others, but not *integrity*. It is arguably the most important word in weight loss. Think about it: you set a weight-loss goal, select a diet, and embark on the journey of becoming a fat loser. Any violation of the plan or promises you made to yourself is a breach of integrity. I think weight-loss and medical professionals avoid addressing this issue because it's a highly emotional concept, another example of allowing emotion to cloud our judgment and impede our progress. The truth is if you break the promises you've made to yourself, you're violating your own integrity. Do this enough times and you'll stop believing your own promises.

This slope is dangerous and slippery because once the integrity of a promise is breached, the strength of the promise is never the same. This is one reason yo-yo dieters often suffer from low self-esteem. They no longer believe their own words, and it erodes the reputation they have with themselves. This issue can also carry over to others. You tell them you're going to become a fat loser over and over, until one day after years of lies, they stop believing you.

The only important question in this equation asks, "Are you a person of integrity or not?" It's a zero-sum, in-your-face, we all have to answer. The bad news is most of us have violated our own integrity in the weight-loss process. I certainly have. The good news says today is a new day and you can start over from scratch. Use this gift to build confidence and self-esteem as you lose weight. It gives you multiple benefits for maintaining your integrity.

> *"Fat people have integrity issues when it comes to weight loss. Fat losers keep their promises."*

Critical Thinking Question

ARE YOU A PERSON OF INTEGRITY OR NOT?

Action Step

Detail your diet plan at least one day in advance so you know the foods you'll be eating at every meal, and make no exceptions until you reach your ideal weight.

MENTAL-TOUGHNESS STRATEGY #33

BECOME COMMITTED

At its root, dieting is a battle of wills. It's you against yourself, the ultimate contest. It's the old you who wants to keep the comfortable eating habits versus the new you who's struggling to emerge and give birth to a more healthful way of living. Critical thinking suggests that the odds are clearly in favor of the old you with your ingrained eating habits and food choices. The new you becomes the underdog swimming upstream trying to stay alive long enough to break the old habits keeping you fat, sluggish, and unhealthy. This struggle is a dogfight, and the new you is a mini-Dachshund in the ring with a German shepherd.

The new you has a chance if you begin strong with some early weight-loss results that motivate you to keep fighting. It all boils down to commitment, and how much you want to be fit. There's no way to sugar-coat this: you're either one hundred percent committed or you're going to lose the struggle. Walk in the ring with a ninety-nine percent commitment and you're defeated. Remember, your diet is not a toy and you are not a child. Until you make a serious, full-blown commitment, you will always be fat, and if you wait too long, you will dig your own grave. This isn't pretty, but it is reality. The good news says there is still time to save yourself. Forget about all the other times you made a weak commitment and failed. The past is dead, but you're not. You still have time to turn it around, but remember that the clock is ticking. Decide to dedicate yourself to this process for the next ninety days and see what happens.

---

*"**Becoming a fat loser is an all-or-nothing proposition.**
Commit to it one hundred percent and succeed
or commit to it ninety-nine percent and fail."*

Critical Thinking Question

ON A SCALE OF 1-7, 7 AS THE MOST COMMITTED, HOW COMMITTED ARE YOU TO BECOMING A FAT LOSER?

Action Step

Draft a written statement declaring your full one hundred percent commitment to remaining compliant on your diet for at least the next thirty days. Read it every day and show it to as many people as possible to increase your commitment.

MENTAL-TOUGHNESS STRATEGY #34

ANALYZE YOUR BELIEFS

Every personal-development and self-help expert in the world agrees on at least one aspect of psychological performance: beliefs drive human behavior. If you want to change your results, first examine your beliefs. This is the place I started when I began my journey to becoming a fat loser, and it's effective. As I scrutinized my beliefs of eating and exercising, I was shocked to discover the number of limiting, fat-person beliefs I had about food, eating, and dieting. For example, I thought the only foods I could really enjoy were junk foods. The idea of enjoying a healthful meal was foreign to me. I also believed diets were short-term, binge-oriented starvation systems that you endured until you lost the weight you wanted. And these were only a few of the negative beliefs driving my behavior and making me fat.

Once I did this belief analysis, however, I understood the reason I was growing fatter every month. I had the same experience with money. The millionaires I interviewed taught me their beliefs about money; I compared them to mine and realized the reason they were rich and I was poor. It's not rocket science, but it's just as powerful. Most people never take the time to analyze their beliefs, and as a result, they're essentially running on autopilot driven by beliefs they are unaware they have. The same is true for exercise, which contributes to twenty percent of your success. When I analyzed my beliefs about exercise, I shared many beliefs with fit people, such as exercise is an important component of life and should be done consistently. My beliefs around exercise probably saved me from being obese. After you examine your beliefs in these areas, ask yourself if they are helping or hurting you. If you're fat, I promise that many of your beliefs in this area are a major part of the problem. Luckily, beliefs can be changed through upgrading so they serve your best interests. It's a simple method of re-wiring your brain for success.

"Beliefs are the engine of all behavior. Fat people grow fat through beliefs, and fat losers grow fit the same way. It's the same strategy with different beliefs."

Critical Thinking Question

WHEN IT COMES TO DIETING, ARE YOUR BELIEFS CONGRUENT WITH YOUR GOAL OF BECOMING A FAT LOSER?

Action Step

Identify your five most dominant beliefs about dieting and exercising and upgrade them to reflect your new level of thinking.

MENTAL-TOUGHNESS STRATEGY #35

STOP BEING STUPID

How many diets have you tried and failed to complete? How long has this been going on? What's the point of wasting time making promises you can't keep? That's stupid and it needs to stop. Don't feel bad; I've done the same stupid things as you and so have ninety-nine percent of the people reading this book. The collective stupidity we've demonstrated is staggering, and I quit the stupid group years ago. I'm suggesting you do the same. If only everyone in America would agree to do this, we'd have the fittest population in the world. Just to prove the popularity of being stupid about fitness, let's examine global statistics.

According to the World Health Organization, 1.4 billion people worldwide are overweight or obese. That number speaks to some serious stupidity. Why are so many smart people acting stupid? Because eating junk food tastes great, and relaxing on the sofa every night drinking beer and eating pizza is a blast! It will drain the life out of you in the short term and kill you in the long term, but in the present moment, it rocks! The fat people of the world aren't stupid for seeking pleasure from food; they're stupid for thinking it won't catch up to them.

I had a friend who was a world-class professional speaker and self-made multi-millionaire. He was a tremendous talent who lived a wonderful rags-to-riches story. He traveled all over the world delivering speeches at the largest corporate conventions and the audiences loved him. As he grew older and fatter, though, he gave up on dieting, thinking he *could beat the system*. He weighed more than 400 pounds the last time I saw him. In business, he was smart, but in his personal life, he was stupid, and now he's dead. And he was only forty-nine years old when he died of a massive heart attack. Stupidity about your health isn't a joke. It kills. If you're fifteen-to-twenty pounds overweight, stop being stupid or you'll be fifty pounds overweight and in serious danger. If you're fifty pounds or more overweight, you need to stop being stupid before you drop dead. You're playing Russian roulette with your life. Put the doughnut down, get off the sofa, and go to the gym. How many more fat people do we need to bury in a box at fifty before you believe you could be next? Be smart, embrace fitness, and become an example to other fat people instead of a cautionary tale. The world needs more fit people. Why not get smart and become one of them?

"Fat people become fat by being stupid about eating and exercising. Fat losers wise up, grow tough, and are living proof that stupidity can be overcome."

Critical Thinking Question

YOU'RE A SMART PERSON. AREN'T YOU TIRED OF ACTING STUPID?

Action Step

Post a sign on your refrigerator that reads: "Stop Being Stupid!"

MENTAL-TOUGHNESS STRATEGY #36

BEGIN DELAYING GRATIFICATION

One of the best things in life is instant pleasure. Being hired for the first job for which you apply, falling in love with the first person you date, or eating a hot-fudge sundae, and feeling it ooze down your throat. Immediate pleasure is hard to resist. The only thing better than instant pleasure is the deep sense of psychological satisfaction and emotional fulfillment you experience through delayed gratification. We've all experienced it in one way or another. Perhaps it was graduating from college, finally making partner at a law firm, or just watching your kids grow into the independent adults you taught them to be.

For me, it was making my first million. I was disappointed I didn't become the tennis champion I'd worked so hard to become, and once that dream ended, I was lost. I eventually decided to direct my mental energy toward being financially independent, and when I achieved that goal, I felt as if it *erased* my failure in tennis. Like everyone with a dream, I wanted it overnight but all I received was failure. After years of losing money, being penniless, and frustrated, the tide finally turned and my dreams were fulfilled. I can remember exactly where I was when it happened, and the way it felt. That was many years ago, but the feeling of victory has grown sweeter over time, and that's typical of goals and dreams for which you have to fight for, isn't it? The goals that come easy are forgotten quickly, but the ones you for which you have to fight stay with you. Here's my point: I hope you become a fat loser overnight and sculpt the body of your dreams in record time.

It usually doesn't work that way, but I wish you the quickest victory with the least amount of suffering. While hoping for the best, however, I suggest you prepare for the worst. Be ready to sacrifice instant pleasure for delayed gratification. The good news is you'll probably appreciate it more than someone experiencing overnight success. Your gradual and eventual victory will be a source of pride for the rest of your life. The old adage states: "There is no victory without struggle, for they are one in the same."

"Everyone strives for the quick victory, but only the mentally tough have the wherewithal to withstand the frustration and failure of a drawn-out battle before ultimately succeeding."

Critical Thinking Question

ARE YOU MENTALLY AND EMOTIONALLY PREPARED TO GO THE DISTANCE, NO MATTER THE LENGTH OF TIME IT REQUIRES TO BECOME A FAT LOSER?

Action Step

Start telling yourself that you're going to stay one hundred percent compliant on your diet and exercise program, but this goal might take longer than you originally planned. This thought will mentally prepare you to expect delaycd gratification.

MENTAL-TOUGHNESS STRATEGY #37

SEE YOURSELF AS A COMEBACK ARTIST

The problem with dieters is the amount of baggage they bring to the battle. They have years of stories about their failure on the peanut, cookie, or star-trek diet. They have let themselves down so many times they're terrified of doing it again. I understand that. It's only human to protect yourself from pain. But the past doesn't equal the future, and the last time has nothing to do with this time. Consciousness is like a moving river: you never step into the same water twice. You're not the same person you were the last time you tried to lose weight, even if it's only been a few weeks. The mind is a marvelous machine that must move forward or die. That's the reason we're always making new distinctions on old concepts, habits, and beliefs. Think about it for a moment: what does the concept of love mean to you now compared to twenty years ago? Love didn't change, but your consciousness did, and as a result, you've evolved to create new perceptions of it.

Winners in every walk of life learn to embrace their failures and see themselves as comeback artists. The issue that most people see as a loss, one-time losers see as an opportunity to learn, return, and try again. The comeback artist who refuses to quit always wins eventually because quitting is never an option. The more times these comeback artists fail, the more they learn. The more they learn, the smarter they become. The smarter they become, the closer they move to their goal.

I know you've failed at dieting before, so what, big deal. Join the club. We have a great many members. Instead of crying in your beer, I want you to toughen up and say, "I'm a come-back artist." If you develop this mindset, nothing can stop you.

> *"Fat people see themselves as failures. Fat losers see themselves as comeback artists, no matter how many times they fail."*

Critical Thinking Question

HOW CAPABLE ARE YOU OF BREAKING THE CYCLE OF DIETING FAILURE AND CREATING A COMEBACK STORY?

Action Step

Start telling yourself everyday that you're a comeback artist and you'll keep coming back no matter how long it takes to succeed.

MENTAL-TOUGHNESS STRATEGY #38

BEGIN BEING COACHABLE

As someone who had the privilege of receiving world-class coaching from ages six-to- twenty-two, and eventually coaching some of the greatest athletes in the world, I can tell you with some authority that there's a huge difference between being *coached* and being *coachable*. Anyone can be coached, but to be coachable requires a willingness to empty your mind of everything you think you know and be completely open to making changes. There is no place for ego, argument, or disagreement. Either trust the coach or fire him. This requirement applies to being coached in any area of life, including weight loss.

I'm the co-founder of the *Think Rich Team*; a group of mental-toughness coaches who work worldwide with the goal of helping people become fat losers. We call it the *Think Rich Team* because the more clients the coaches help, the more money they earn. Our goal centers on helping ten million people become fit through mental-toughness coaching while creating a thousand millionaire coaches. The mental-toughness coaches' greatest challenge is the "coach-ability" of their clients. If you're going to become a fat loser on your own, you don't need to worry about this. But if you have a mental toughness coach, fitness trainer, or other kind of coach guiding you, for goodness sakes learn to be *coachable*. It will speed your weight loss significantly and prevent your coach from jumping off a bridge. The following steps to being coachable are simple:

1. Listen to the coach.

2. Do what the coach tells you.

3. Don't argue with the coach.

4. You're the student and he or she is the coach.

5. Don't confuse number four.

These simple guidelines are all it takes. Therefore, consider finding a coach to assist you in expediting the weight-loss process. If it works, you'll be happy you did it. If it doesn't, you can always fire him or her and go it alone.

"Let go of your ego and hire a coach to help you become a fat loser. If becoming fit was so easy and you were good at it, wouldn't you have done it on your own by now?

Critical Thinking Question

ARE YOU ALLOWING PRIDE AND EGO TO INTERFERE WITH YOUR COACHING?

Action Step

Email Dawn Andrews at dawn@ssnlive.org to see if you qualify for free mental toughness coaching for weight loss.

MENTAL-TOUGHNESS STRATEGY #39

STOP TALKING AND START WORKING

Everyone talks a good game. It's easy to bloviate about becoming a fat loser, becoming fit, and thereby changing your life. I've done my share of big talking, too, so I'm not one to judge. That being said, as you embark on this new journey to optimal health and fitness, ask yourself: am I more interested in talking about this or doing it? This question sounds like an obvious one, but when you dig deeper, it's not. Talking to yourself and others about losing weight gives you the sense that you're on your way to feeling good again, both physically and mentally. Before you even select a diet, you feel a sense of hope and even accomplishment, although you haven't done anything but *talk about it*. I'll give you a parallel example: I am paid to give speeches at conventions. It's a fulfilling career that many people worldwide dream about pursuing. Approximately 3,000 of those people call our office every year in Florida, wanting to break into the business. We refer them to the Bill Gove Speech Workshop, which is the most successful professional speaker-training course in the world. We also offer them training courses on audio and video. In 2013, a Minneapolis author, Elliot Saltzman, wrote a book entitled *How to Become a Million Dollar Speaker: The Steve Siebold Story*, and we advise them to read that book as a resource.

The people who have been calling our office for the past eighteen years all say the same thing: their dream is to become a speaker, and they'll do anything to accomplish it. Some of them are so passionate about their dream that they cry on the phone. They talk convincingly about their dream, but only about five percent of them follow through. Some of them won't even invest in a twenty-dollar book containing many of the answers they're seeking. It's much easier to talk about what you're going to do than it is to do it. Again, I'm an offender as well. I've been telling myself for almost forty years that I'm going to dedicate myself to studying guitar seriously, yet four decades later I'm still a three-chord novice.

We're all experts at talking, and the question still remains, will this time be different for you? Are you really ready to work and become fit, or are you just spouting off about it because it sounds good? If you've been a big talker in the past but not a big doer, forgive yourself and start over. You still have time on the clock. I don't know the amount of time. I'm sure James Gandolfini thought he had all the time in the world to become fit, but his time ran out. Don't let that happen to you. We've all talked enough about wanting to be fit. Now it's time to stop talking and start working.

"Talk is easy. Action is tough. Go to work."

Critical Thinking Question

CAN YOU REALLY SUPPORT YOUR BIG TALK WITH BIG ACTION, OR ARE YOU JUST ANOTHER BLOW-HARD?

Action Step

Every time you talk to yourself or others about your diet or fitness goals, analyze whether the action you're taking is congruent with the words you're saying.

MENTAL-TOUGHNESS STRATEGY #40

DO THE WORK

In the 1970s when I was competing around the country in junior tennis, I had one of the top coaches in the world. He was a brutal-dictator-type coach like Vince Lombardi. He had about twenty national champions in our group, and it was equivalent to being in the Marines. We practiced for three-to-four hours after school, and then ran wind sprints as well as long distance. He made us run three miles for time, and if you didn't run it under eighteen minutes, you had to do it over. The average age in the group was fourteen. I was ten. The youngest was nine and her name was Andrea.

I remember one time when all of us were running sprints; the person coming in last had to run it again in front of the group before continuing. Andrea was only nine years old, and she was fast, but a few other young kids and I were taller and a little faster, so she was always last. One day, in front of ten to fifteen of our parents, the coach kept telling Andrea to keep sprinting, which she did, until she vomited all over the court. She started crying, and the coach said, "Go cry to your mother, she's right there. But if you walk off my court, you'll never walk back on." Through a face full of tears Andrea stood up and kept running.

Of course the parents were outraged and threatened to pull their kids off the team. The coach responded by saying, "Go ahead, this team has a three-year waiting list. I'll replace your kid in twenty minutes." And it was true. He was the best.

Almost all the kids on that team made it to the pros. The most successful of us all, though, was little Andrea. Andrea Yeager shocked the world by becoming the youngest quarter-finalist in the history of Wimbledon and eventually climbed to #2 in the world.

I haven't seen that coach for nearly forty years, but the lessons he taught me and the rest of the team changed our lives, the greatest of which was simply to do the work whether you feel like it or not. He used to say that everyone wants the glory of success, but few are willing to pay the price when the pain begins and everyone else has gone home. Once the excitement of starting your new diet turns to cravings, fatigue, and hunger pangs, the real game begins. You don't have to set weight-loss records or become the next supermodel. All you have to do is work, step-by-step, day-by-day, hour-by-hour, and meal-by-meal. There's not much glory or recognition in doing the work, but remember that every dog has its day and yours is coming. Pay the price today and reap the rewards tomorrow. You've set the goal and selected your diet. All that's left is the work.

"Successful dieting means doing the work. Flashy diets and extreme exercises are mere distractions. To become a fat loser stop talking about it and just do the work."

Critical Thinking Question

ARE YOU STILL NEGOTIATING THE PRICE OF SUCCESS OR ARE YOU READY TO GO TO WORK AND MAKE IT HAPPEN?

Action Step

When you become hungry, tired, frustrated, or impatient in the weight-loss process, tell yourself to stay focused and do the work. There is no easy way out.

MENTAL-TOUGHNESS STRATEGY #41

EMBRACE THE DISCIPLINE

Something is fundamentally motivating about being on the path to success. It doesn't even seem to matter the kind of success you're seeking. The fulfillment the warrior feels when she is fighting the war is unique and difficult to explain. It's unlike any other form of pleasure. It's a deep psychological satisfaction that accompanies fighting the good fight. It's a nonlinear experience to derive pleasure from pain, yet we've all *felt it*. It's the reason people run marathons, lift weights, and practice martial arts. The beginning starts off as pain but evolves into euphoria difficult to quantify, yet easy to feel. It's a sense that you're giving a goal everything you have and leaving it all on the field. No excuses, no regrets, just pure performance and positive energy.

I remember struggling ardently to become a professional speaker, working eighteen-hour days, and sleeping in my office. I was penniless, frustrated, and exhausted for the first two years. My wife and I were living in a ten-foot by ten-foot room in my parent's house, working like dogs and getting nowhere. Sometimes we'd meet up at the local bowling alley at eleven or twelve at night for a drink after working all day and evening. We were frustrated and exhausted. Sometimes we'd laugh and sometimes cry, but we were in the fight of our lives and we knew it. We'd grit our teeth and say, "Someday we'll be millionaires and laugh at this." Then we'd return to our room, sleep a few hours, and start the routine over again, seven days a week for two years. I'm sure we took a day or two off during that time, but neither of us can recall it.

When you're that engaged in the fight, it's difficult to think about anything else. It wasn't fun, but we both learned to embrace the discipline it required to realize our dream. It wasn't perfect or pretty, it was a real-world fight that seemed as though it would never end, until one day, it did. And when success finally happened, it didn't rain, it *poured*. And that's typical of success, isn't it? You fight like a dog and nothing happens for a long time, and just as you're about to give up, the dream becomes reality.

Becoming a fat loser is no different. I'm not asking you simply to endure the discipline; I'm suggesting that you *embrace* it. Stare it down. Look it straight in the eye. When you feel those late-night hunger pangs and cravings, I want you to experience them fully. Think about the way it feels in your stomach and your mind. That's the feeling of victory telling you if you can do this, you can anything. And you'll be right. Instead of fearing the pain or avoiding it, embrace it and the discipline required to continue. You'll start looking in the mirror and seeing the person you really are and were always meant to be.

> *"Fat people fear the pain of dieting. Fat losers look pain straight in the eye and say, 'I'm stronger than you. You cannot defeat me'."*

Critical Thinking Question

ARE YOU READY TO EMBRACE THE DISCIPLINE IT TAKES TO SUCCEED?

Action Step

Make a list of the five biggest sacrifices it takes to diet successfully and the five biggest benefits of succeeding. Now examine the two lists and determine whether the benefits outweigh the sacrifices.

MENTAL-TOUGHNESS STRATEGY #42

BEGIN DOING THE WORK IT TAKES TO SUCCEED

There's a time-honored secret among the most successful people in the world. It's not common among the masses, yet anyone is capable of doing it. The secret is doing the work it takes to win. When I say this, I don't mean putting in a good effort. Most of us do that. I'm saying doing *the work it takes* to succeed, no matter the price. Most people will fight to succeed, and others will do their best. But what if your best isn't good enough? That's the time you call on the psychological reserves most people don't know they have. This primal, all-or-nothing, winner-take-all mentality won't accept anything but victory at any cost.

An example of this mindset occurred back in the 1500s when General Cortez of Cuba was invading Mexico by boat. They landed on the beach and Cortez ordered them to "burn the boats." This order gave his men no way to retreat. They'd either win or die.

This mentality may seem appropriate for war but extreme for weight loss, but it isn't. You see; weight loss is a *personal* war. It pits your old habits against the new ones, and the outcome may determine whether you live or die. No hyperbole. Fat kills. And even if you're among the group with only a modest amount of weight to lose, your battle amounts to quality of life. Do you really want to stare at your bloated body in the mirror for the rest of your life? Do you really want to feel ashamed every time you see your distorted face in photographs? Being twenty pounds overweight may not kill you, but it will certainly diminish your quality of life, not to mention the psychological aspects of being *moderately* fat. It's a confidence-killer and self-esteem destroyer.

The key centers on adopting the whatever-it-takes philosophy and making it happen. This attitude is the secret of champions, and now it's yours. You've not only known this secret your whole life but also used it in one way or another. Now it's time to use it again to become fit.

> *"Doing the work it takes to succeed is a strategy, philosophy, and mindset. The result is an unstoppable performer."*

Critical Thinking Question

ARE YOU READY TO EMBRACE THE DISCIPLINE IT TAKES TO SUCCEED?

Action Step

Make a list of the five reasons you'll do whatever it takes to become a fat loser.

MENTAL-TOUGHNESS STRATEGY #43

BEGIN BELIEVING IN YOURSELF

Building a support team is a smart strategy. The added energy and team-like feeling will help propel you through the process. At the end of the day, however, when everyone goes home and it's only you and the scale, your success will amount to the belief you have in yourself. This belief is difficult if you've failed on diets in the past, but it's critical to sustaining your level of motivation. Can you become a fat loser without believing in yourself? Of course you can. In a biochemical process like dieting, your belief is technically not required, but it does help to keep you on the path. People who lack self-belief often cheat on their diets because deep down they believe they're going to fail.

How do you create self-belief if you've never succeeded in dieting? You brainwash yourself to believe it. Brainwashing is merely a process that can be used to help or hurt us. Ever wonder how it's possible that eighty-five percent of Americans believe so strongly in a God they've never seen? It's simple. We've been bombarded with this message since infancy. If you tell a human being anything from infancy for eighteen consecutive years, that person will believe it. Whether it's true or not is irrelevant. The human mind is highly susceptible to consistent messaging.

That's the way advertisers brainwash us into buying their products. One of the most successful examples is the jewelry industry's commercial that states, "The engagement ring you select should be the equal to three months of your salary." You might say what I said, "According to whom?" You already know the answer, according to the jewelry industry. Recommending that a young couple spend three months' salary on a ring is borderline criminal. If the groom earns $40,000 per year, he's supposed to spend $10,000 on an engagement ring? Do you really believe he has $10,000 to spend? No, so he goes into debt to buy it. This is bad advice, but when you ask people about the amount appropriate to spend on a ring, they'll often repeat this advertising gimmick. That's the power of programming.

Using programming to build your own belief works in the same way. Start telling yourself every day, as often as possible, that you are dedicated and disciplined on your diet, and that you *always* exercise. You tell yourself that you have what it takes to be healthy and fit. You tell yourself that when you focus on what you want, you never miss. Get the idea? Its positive programming designed to strengthen your level of belief. If you repeat these messages long enough and strong enough, you'll be amazed that you start acting accordingly.

"People in power have always used psychological programming to control the masses. Use the same programming technique to make your mind believe anything that serves your best interests."

Critical Thinking Question

ON A SCALE OF 1-7, 7 AS THE MOST, HOW MUCH DO YOU BELIEVE IN YOURSELF?

Action Step

Start listening to a CD album entitled The Making of a Million Dollar Mind. This CD will give you a head-start on creating messages that build self-belief.
www.milliondollarmind.com

MENTAL-TOUGHNESS STRATEGY #44

FOCUS ON THE FUTURE

Imagine what your life will be like as a fit and healthy fat loser. Imagine the way you'll feel waking up in the morning with a body ready to deliver more energy in a day than it used to deliver in a week. How will being fit impact your relationships? How will it affect your financial life? How will it benefit your overall happiness? Being fit will have a positive effect on everything you do and everyone around you.

After I lost the forty pounds I'd gained over a few years, I couldn't *believe* the difference I felt. Physically, mentally, and emotionally the benefits were beyond my wildest expectations. I felt so good about myself. I felt as if I'd conquered my junk-food habit and could do anything. Over the next few years, everything in my life improved, and the catalyst was the simple act of dropping forty pounds in twelve weeks. You're going to feel the same, and you'll be shocked at how good this is going to be.

As a means of test-driving your future as a fit person, write a letter to a friend. Date this letter five years in the future and tell your friend about everything you want to happen in your life as if it already has. Explain in detail what it's like to be physically fit and feeling great. Describe the way your body feels in clothes and the great feeling you have when looking in the mirror. Describe looking and feeling good, and your life as a fit person. Notice the way you feel as you write this letter. What you're experiencing is your future in the present.

> *"Your future as a fat loser is only one decision away. It will alter your entire life."*

Critical Thinking Question

HAVE YOU CONSIDERED THE IDEA THAT YOUR FUTURE IS BEING SHAPED BY YOUR PERFORMANCE ON THIS DIET?

Action Step

Talk to someone who went from fat to fit and ask that person about the way it impacted his or her life.

MENTAL-TOUGHNESS STRATEGY #45

EAT CONGRUENTLY

When I started my diet, I didn't consider the foods I was eating as incongruent with the way I wanted to feel. In other words, I wanted to feel good physically, mentally, and emotionally after a meal, but my junk-food diet had left me with less energy, more guilt, and the emotional frustration that I was working against my own best interests. I always loved pizza, but it gave me heartburn. I always craved chips, but they made me feel bloated. Ice cream and candy tasted great, but left me with a stomachache. I know that logically these effects make sense.

Obviously these kinds of foods make us fat, and in order to lose it, we have to give them up. If dieting were that logical, it would be easy. Dieting, while a logical biochemical process, is often emotional to the dieter. I remember feeling addicted to those junk foods, and while I knew it was in my best interest to break the addiction, I *struggled* with it. I found I had to ask myself questions at every meal: is this food congruent with my goals? Are the effects congruent with the way I want to feel? I know it tastes good, but will it bring me closer to my goals? If this sounds like a fourth-grade process, it is.

Remember, though, weight loss is simple but not easy, and the more tools you have at your disposal the easier it will be. I started saying *no* to incongruent foods and *yes* to the foods that served me nutritionally. I was initially disappointed when I decided to eat the salmon or salad instead of the pizza or cookie, but after I was full, I experienced a deep sense of accomplishment. The more I focused on this congruency question, the more weight I lost. Therefore, take time before making every food selection to answer the congruency question. It will help keep you focused and on track.

"Congruency is critical to success. If you say one thing and do another, it's difficult to achieve goals. Remain congruent and success will follow."

Critical Thinking Question

ARE YOUR LAST THREE MEALS CONGRUENT WITH YOUR GOAL OF BECOMING A FAT LOSER?

Action Step

For the next twenty-four hours, carefully analyze the way you make food choices and examine your thoughts along the way. This unconscious process created the body you have today.

MENTAL-TOUGHNESS STRATEGY #46

LISTEN TO FIT PEOPLE

After interviewing fit people, eating meals with them, and working out with them over the course of two years, I was shocked at the amount of information I learned. These people are so consciously aware of the food they put into their mouths, it's no wonder they're so fit.

The same applies to exercise. Missing an exercise session to a fit person is like failing to show up for work. It rarely happens. I should have known that fit people see the world differently, but I honestly didn't. I thought because I was an athlete, we'd share the same views about eating and exercising. We didn't. One of us was thinking like a fat person and I'll bet you can guess which one?

Amazing was their attention to detail in their meal choices. They carefully analyzed portion sizes, ingredients, calories, salt content, and other facts. I kept thinking to myself, *I've never even thought about any of this, much less done anything about it.* Like most people, I just ate the foods that tasted good, and the bigger the portion size, the better. If my stomach wasn't bulging by the time I finished, I ordered more. At first I thought the fit people were extreme in their details, but when I worked out with them and witnessed their energy level, I changed my mind. My experience with fit people forever altered the way I think about food and the way I consume it. Find someone who is fit and ask that person the way he or she did it. It may surprise and inspire you.

"Fat people follow fat people. Fit people follow fit people. Decide on the person to follow based on the results you're seeking."

Critical Thinking Question

ARE YOU LISTENING TO FAT OR FIT PEOPLE ABOUT DIETING?

Action Step

Make a list of all the fit people you know and set a date to share a meal or workout session with each one of them. The exposure to their thinking and behavioral habits will have a positive impact on you.

MENTAL-TOUGHNESS STRATEGY #47

DIET FOR FUN

I know your thoughts: Siebold has lost it. Dieting is *not* fun. Well, yes and no. *No*, it's not your *normal* kind of fun, but *yes*, it is fun. My answer simply means being fat is detrimental. It makes you look and feel bad. It costs you money, credibility, energy, vitality, sex, self-esteem, confidence, and more. Being fit is the opposite, especially in a country where seventy percent of the population is overweight or obese. Being fit makes you look and feel like a winner. And *the fun of dieting* awaits you when you succeed. When was the last time you looked good in a bathing suit? Isn't it *fun* thinking about how sexy you're going to look the next time you hit the pool or the beach? How about shopping for clothes? When was the last time you tried on clothes that were too large for your lean body? Clothes-shopping is fun for fit people. They can buy straight off the rack and everything fits. When was the last time you bought a pair of tight jeans? Do you remember the way it felt to slide them on without having to inhale and hold your breath?

How about seeing old friends at your high school reunion? How much fun will it be to buy a beautiful dress or a new suit to slide over your svelte body and watch everyone's jaw drop? How about regaining the sex drive you had when you were fit? Fit people can't wait to remove their clothes. I'll stop there, but I think you get the point. I send my apologies to those who feel insulted by my shallow scenarios. I'll add something more substantial for you: isn't it fun knowing you won't drop dead in the street and leave your family fending for themselves?

Discipline by nature isn't enjoyable, but imagining the future rewards of it certainly can be. Bruce Jenner, the 1976 Olympic Decathlon Champion, said the one thing that kept him training so hard was imagining his victory, running into the Olympic stadium, and taking a victory lap while carrying the American flag around the track. He dreamed that fantasy for years while enduring torturous training, and on race day millions of us watched as he circled the track with the victory flag.

I'm not trying to persuade you to be positive about dieting. Alone, we know it isn't any more fun than training for a race. However, when you combine it with what it will do for you in the future and train yourself to imagine it, that's when the fun begins.

"Fat people have fun eating. Fat losers have fun dreaming of the day they'll reach their fitness goals and realize their potential."

Critical Thinking Question

WOULD YOU RATHER HAVE FUN WITH FOOD OR FUN AS A HEALTHY, SEXY, ENERGETIC HUMAN BEING?

Action Step

Make a list of all the things that will change in your life when you become fit, and rank them in order of the amount of enjoyment.

MENTAL-TOUGHNESS STRATEGY #48

DIET FOR PROFIT

Before I gained weight and lost it, I'd never have believed in the correlation between fitness and money. It's obviously a nonlinear connection, but it's as *powerful* as anything I've ever seen. On the surface it makes sense. Become fit, gain energy, work more, and earn more. Simple enough, but it goes beyond that. Becoming fit transforms your entire psychological makeup. It not only makes you feel good physically, but also mentally. It changes your attitude and outlook on everything because you begin seeing the world through the eyes of success, abundance, and opportunity. For example, have you wondered why some people seem to go from success to success, from one victory to another, as though they have a guardian angel guiding them? There's actually a much simpler explanation. It's called *psychological momentum*.

The principle states that every victory moves you one step closer to the next, and the more you succeed, the stronger the momentum becomes. The mind is a powerful tool, and people who believe they can win often do because they perform like a person who can't fail. Earning large amounts of money begins with the belief that you're capable of it. When you're fat, sluggish, and depressed, however, you see the world and everything in it through that lens. It looks like a dark place where the best strategy is to seek security and save every penny you earn. When you view the world through the eyes of a fit, healthy, happy person, however, *all you can see is opportunity*. The world doesn't change, you do.

Playing it safe is no longer your priority; realizing your potential is your new goal. Instead of settling on hitting singles, you start swinging for the fences, and you only need one home run to be rich. Don't believe me? Give it a try and see if I'm exaggerating. Think of it this way: how many obese rich people do you know? Everything in life affects everything else. Success breed's success and the rich do become richer. You've heard these platitudes so many times because they're true. The next time you reach for that shorty doughnut, consider your financial cost and prepare a protein shake instead. Your financial advisor would surely approve.

"Dieting for profit might be the highest paid work in the world, but only the most critical thinkers will make the connection."

Critical Thinking Question

HAVE YOU MADE THE CONNECTION BETWEEN PHYSICAL FITNESS AND MONEY?

Action Step

Make a list of five ways you believe money is connected to fitness.

MENTAL-TOUGHNESS STRATEGY #49

FORGIVE YOURSELF

I know you feel bad about getting fat. You let yourself go and feel lousy about it. I've been there, and so have most Americans. My advice is to let it go. Wallowing in self-pity is a waste of time and a bad habit to boot. Forgive yourself for being sloppy and begin resolving the issue. One difference between winners and losers in life is that losers focus on the past and winners focus on the present and future. Today you're in a fight, moving toward a better tomorrow. That's all that counts. Yesterday is gone and it isn't coming back. When I gained forty pounds, I had moments of thinking like a loser. Not a FAT loser, just a *loser*. I thought about my tennis days when I was a physical specimen and couldn't wait to remove my shirt at the pool. Boy oh boy, I would say to myself, if I were only twenty-two again, this weight-gain wouldn't have happened.

Now that I'm older, my metabolism is slowing down and it's more difficult to stay fit. In case you're wondering, these are the words of a *loser*. Luckily, I'd catch myself during these weak moments and snap back into winner's mode, sounding more like *"I should have been paying closer attention to my weight. I'm older now and I need to be more careful about the foods I'm eating. No big deal, I made a mistake, and I'll solve the problem. I was the problem and now I'm the solution. I know the things to do and I'll do them. Nothing can stop me. Fitness is on its way."*

See the difference? When you stop beating yourself up and begin focusing on becoming fit, everything changes. Now you're thinking and talking like a winner, and winners rule the world.

The only people who hate hearing that are the losers. So stop crying about the terrible drama you've experienced. It's ancient history. Instead, think about your amazing future. That's the place on which to focus.

"Losers can't forgive themselves for getting fat. Winners can."

Critical Thinking Question

HAVE YOU FORGIVEN YOURSELF FOR BECOMING FAT?

Action Step

Build the winner's habit of letting go of the past. Life is short and winners stay focused on the present while planning for the future.

MENTAL-TOUGHNESS STRATEGY #50

KNOW YOUR WHY

There's an old saying in the world of peak performance: "Without knowing why you're doing something, the how doesn't matter." This applies especially when you're tackling big goals like becoming fit after being fat for years. So I'll just ask you point blank: do you know the reason you're pursuing this goal? Answering this question, I made a list of the reasons why I needed to change my eating habits and regain the fitness I'd enjoyed all of my life. The heart of it was that being fat felt unnatural. I'd never been fat before, and I felt as if I were living in someone else's body, living someone else's life. I attended the wedding of a friend I hadn't seen in years and people barely recognized me. My ego was bruised and vanity rose to the forefront.

I was accustomed to people complimenting my body, and I didn't like the alternative. I know your thoughts: how vain, and you're right. I hated having people pity my bloated body, and when I left the wedding, I acted like a man possessed. I immediately bought health and fitness magazines, cutting out pictures of the bodies I wanted to look like and hung them on the every wall in the house. I wrote a list of positive-programming affirmations and repeated them every day. I visited my doctor and he recommended dieting, so I purchased nutritious food. I increased my workouts at the gym and walked every evening. All I could see was a fit body and the benefits it would bring.

Losing my fit body was like losing my fortune. Once you've had it and lost it, you're pretty intense about regaining it. And the crazy thing is I experienced more benefits becoming fit than I had in the past. I'd never appreciated my fitness because I'd never been fat. Again, it's like money. If you've always been wealthy, it's difficult to appreciate it. But once you lose and regain it, you can fully appreciate it by having experienced the other side. My conclusion, I lost weight to take back my life, not just physically, but mentally and emotionally. That was reason enough for me. How about you? You need to know the reason you're engaging in this weight-loss venture and then you'll fight more soundly when it gets rough. At some point, it's going to become difficult. You need to prepare mentally for the tough times. Let's call it an insurance policy. Once your *why* is answered, the *how* will follow.

"When it comes to big goals and dreams, the why is more important than the how, which requires logic. The why runs on emotion, providing the motivation necessary to succeed."

Critical Thinking Question

WHAT IS THE SINGLE BIGGEST REASON YOU WANT TO BECOME A FAT LOSER?

Action Step

Take a couple of hours and retreat to a quiet place to contemplate your emotional reasons for daring to fight.

MENTAL-TOUGHNESS STRATEGY #51

BECOME OBSESSED WITH SUCCESS

After interviewing more than 1,200 of the most successful people in the country since 1984, I've identified the primary catalyst of their success: winners *love* to win. Champions love to stand in the victory circle. People who know the way to fulfilling their wishes have a healthful obsession with success. At the same time, they *hate* to lose. Failure is never an option to fighters, and it only serves as a launching pad for their inevitable victory. Some of these people are competitive and others are not, but both groups share one thing in common, they won't rest until they succeed.

How much do you want to succeed on your diet? Will you accept defeat or keep moving forward until you achieve your goal? I've found through thirty years of research that most people fail because they half-heartedly want so many things they don't focus on the few goals and dreams that matter most. It's easy to become sidetracked. We've all done it. The winners quickly move back on course and continue rocketing down the road until they succeed. Their obsession is not complicated, but it is profound in its effect on their performance.

When I started competing in junior tennis, I was obsessed with winning. I practiced day and night. My appetite for the game was insatiable, and I only wanted to win matches and improve my skills. I trained at an indoor club near Chicago, and when my lessons were finished for the day, I stood by the front door of the club and asked every person entering if he wanted to play. Most said no because they already had matches, but I learned early on that many partners arrived late, so I asked if I could warm them up with while they waited. This worked ninety percent of the time. I'd hit with them for ten to fifteen minutes while they waited and sometimes for the entire hour if the partner failed to show. This time gave me an extra hour of practice each day, and eventually I started to get good.

While my competitors stayed home at night, I remained at the tennis club until nine o'clock practicing. My obsession eventually made me one the best players in the country for my age group. Everyone who succeeds at some goal has a story like this one, and I'll bet you do, too. Developing a healthful obsession with a goal is a strategy that works. When a winner refuses to be denied, the game is over before it begins. After all, you can't stop a man who won't be stopped. You can't beat a man who won't be beaten. How much do you want to become a fat loser? How important is it? The more you analyze your level of motivation the stronger it'll grow.

"Fat people approach weight loss like a game.

Fat losers approach weight loss like a war."

Critical Thinking Question

ON A SCALE OF 1-7, 7 AS THE MOST, HOW MUCH DO YOU WANT TO BECOME FIT AND HEALTHY?

Action Step

Recall a situation in which you had a goal and became obsessed with achieving it, and ask yourself if you have that same obsession for weight loss.

MENTAL-TOUGHNESS STRATEGY #52

BUILD NEW HABITS

When you analyze the weight-loss process, it amounts to breaking bad habits and building new ones. This, of course, is easier said than done. Breaking decades of old, ingrained habits is like trying to take over Fort Knox: there's going to be a battle. When I started my first diet and began analyzing my poor eating habits, I discovered my biggest problem was junk food. While growing up, we had separate cookie and candy drawers, and both were always full of multiple varieties. When I married and told my wife this story, she said, "You're lucky you don't weigh 300 pounds," and that was the end of the cookie and candy drawers. Of course I hid a few Bit O Honey and Snickers bars in the bottom drawer of my desk in case of emergency. I also sneaked in some sugar cookies to make sure I covered all the food groups. It was never really a problem because I was young and worked out every day. Then one day, I woke up to forty extra pounds and had to examine the habits that got me there. I did an objective analysis of my habits and found the following:

1. I overeat when I'm celebrating.

2. I crave candy because I ate it on a regular basis.

3. Whenever I drive someplace, taking more than fifteen minutes, I stop for fast food.

4. I eat for entertainment.

5. I eat more when I stay up late.

I think it's easy to see the way my habits made me fat. Once

I identified them, I had to break them. It wasn't easy, but taking it day-by-day helped and eventually it became easier. Then I had to replace each one with a new, healthful habit. This habit-making-and-breaking process must be completed for long-term weight loss. Can you see the way your habits created your weight problem? Do you know what triggers them? Once you identify and replace them with new empowering habits, you'll be on your way to fat-loser success.

"Fat people form bad eating habits. Fat losers identify their bad habits and replace them with healthy ones."

Critical Thinking Question

ON A SCALE OF 1-7, 7 AS THE MOST PROBLEMATIC, HOW WOULD YOU RANK YOUR WORST EATING HABITS?

Action Step

Make a list of your five worst eating and exercise habits, and another list of the five habits you need to develop to become a fat loser.

MENTAL-TOUGHNESS STRATEGY #53

BECOME HAPPY THROUGH FITNESS

Walk into any American health club and you'll see some of the happiest people on the planet. Something about being in great shape generates happiness. Maybe it's the extra energy or the muscle tone. Maybe it's the way your clothes cling to your body just right. Whatever it is, it works, and those working out and watching the food they eat will agree. The fastest way to beat the blues is building a body that looks like a million bucks.

We've all had episodes in our lives in which we struggled with depression. If you live long enough, you'll experience it sooner or later. It seems to be a part of the human condition. Mine happened twenty years ago. Before that, I honestly don't remember being depressed a day in my life. I was always a happy-go-lucky kid and carried it into adulthood. When I saw friends suffering from depression, I genuinely didn't understand it. Then one day, wham! I struggled through a tragedy that seemed to last forever, and I slipped into a severe depression. It was so strange for me, Mister Positive Thinker, to be experiencing such extreme feelings of despair. No matter how hard I tried, I couldn't seem to shake it. This depression lasted for more than two years, and the only thing that alleviated the suffering was working out, running, and improving my fitness.

The exercise served as an antidepressant, and the more I worked out, the better I felt. The more fit I became, the more empowered I felt, and the confidence I gained helped me rebuild my life.

Without the boost that exercise gave me, I don't know if I'd have been as successful. This perk is another benefit of becoming a fat loser. You're going to be happier than you've ever been. Knowing that you set a goal to become fit and achieved it against all odds will serve as a source of pride for life. Being fit and looking fabulous is one thing, but isn't happiness the ultimate benefit? If you think I'm exaggerating the power fitness has on happiness, try it. You won't be disappointed.

"Fat people are disappointed with themselves and depressed about being fat. Fat losers are thrilled with their fitness and happy with themselves."

Critical Thinking Question

ON A SCALE OF 1-7, 7 AS THE MOST IMPORTANT, HOW IMPORTANT A ROLE DOES FITNESS PLAY IN YOUR HAPPINESS?

Action Step

Do some self-analysis on your level of happiness. Would you identify yourself as depressed, mildly depressed, fine, happy, or very happy? No matter the answer, becoming fit will move you to the next level.

MENTAL-TOUGHNESS STRATEGY #54

BECOME BRUTALLY HONEST WITH YOURSELF

A big part of mental-toughness training is moving yourself into objective reality as it relates to the goal you're pursuing. I call it brutal honesty, because from a psychological standpoint, it can be brutal, especially if you're not used to it. If you want to be a better spouse or parent, examine your strengths and weaknesses objectively without emotion clouding your judgment. If you want to earn more money, analyze the beliefs and habits that are holding you back. If you want to become a fat loser, analyze the reasons for becoming fat.

I stopped paying attention to the food I ate. I made excuses, such as my traveling around the world, working eighteen-hour days, and having no time to diet. Another reason was I didn't want to stop eating the junk food I enjoyed. I didn't want to discipline myself about eating because I was experiencing so much stress, frustration, and failure in business that I didn't want to endure any more. That thinking made me fat. You wouldn't think this would be a big surprise, right? Well, it was to me, and that's the power of self-delusion and why being brutally honest and examining objective reality is so important. There's no mystery in this equation, outside of the emotional delusion in which we sometimes operate.

We become fat through bad habits and exacerbate the issue with self-delusion. It's a formula for disaster, and self-delusion on a global scale has created the obesity epidemic. To beat it, a person has to awaken from the drunken stupor that fuels it. The first step includes looking in the mirror and promising yourself not to lie about your weight. Stop inhaling and take a good look at yourself. This isn't fun and you might cry, but do it anyway. If you're going to win this battle, you have to identify the enemy, and *the enemy is you*. The good news is you're also the hero coming to save the day. Take a deep breath and prepare to critique yourself with brutal but loving honesty. Take a hundred percent responsibility for everything you find, but don't beat yourself up. All of us have been where you are or will be in the future. Once you become honest with yourself, the emotional burden of being fat will begin to fade.

"Fat people dodge the reality of being fat.

Fat losers stare it straight in the face."

Critical Thinking Question

ON A SCALE OF 1-7, 7 AS THE CLOSEST, HOW CLOSE ARE YOU TO OPERATING FROM OBJECTIVE REALITY WHEN IT COMES TO YOUR WEIGHT?

Action Step

Decide today to stop fooling yourself about your weight. Whether your daily results are good, bad, or average, avoid deluding yourself.

MENTAL-TOUGHNESS STRATEGY #55

WRITE ABOUT YOUR BODY VISION

If you've ever studied business, you know that any serious start-up has a written plan. A solid business plan averages fifty to a hundred pages of extensive detail on product, budgeting, projections, and so on, plus it usually spans three to five years in the future. Business plans are written for two reasons: one, for potential lenders, such as banks and investors; two, to create clarity, direction, and focus for the entrepreneur or the team starting the business. The funny thing about a business plan is once the door's open and the market responds, the business plan must be altered immediately. All experienced entrepreneurs know this, yet they recognize the importance of the exercise.

You've decided to embark on one of the most important journeys of your life, the road to fitness and optimal health. This goal is more important than any business. All the money and success in the world can't save you from dying fat, only you can. For that reason you need to have a business plan for your body. It doesn't need to be fifty pages long, but it does need to include the details of the image you want to create. For example, my ultimate vision is the body I had when I was playing professional tennis. I was lean and muscular with minimal body-fat. My energy level was off the charts, my body image was healthful, and my confidence was high. That's an overview, which is the first step in writing your body vision.

The next step considers the details, such as describing the way you want your six-pack abs or your legs to look as you shape and sculpt them through exercise. Maybe you're obese and your vision is to be able to tie your own shoes again. Your starting place doesn't matter, only the direction in which you're going. The next part of your written body vision should describe the way you will feel when you arrive at your destination. Waking up every day to a fit body is a wonderful feeling that affects every aspect of your life. It is literally life-changing. Once you've finished your body vision, read it every day to flood your consciousness with these images and emotions, especially during tough times. This exercise will propel you to the professional level of this process. You're no longer playing a game or dabbling in a diet; you're playing to win the ultimate war, the battle of the bulge. You're going to be struck at the way this exercise affects you.

> *"Fat people fantasize about being fit. Fat losers fantasize about being fit while following the diet that will make it happen."*

Critical Thinking Question

DO YOU HAVE A RAZOR-SHARP IMAGE OF THE WAY YOU WANT YOUR BODY TO LOOK?

Action Step

Take an hour this week to write your body vision and read it every day.

MENTAL-TOUGHNESS STRATEGY #56

DEMAND LOGICAL THINKING

Mental-toughness training is learning to control and manipulate your emotions to serve your best interests. A major part of the process is developing the psychological skills to separate logical from emotional thinking. Logic is used for decision-making and emotion for motivation. When it comes to weight loss, logic should steer your food selection, exercise scheduling, weight-loss tracking, and so on. Emotion is used in the role of cheerleader and chief motivator. Reading your body vision, sending a letter to a friend, creating a vision board, and using other motivational tools are all examples of the proper use of emotion in performance. When it comes to following your diet, you must demand logical thinking even when your emotions are tugging at you. That's the time when emotional control or mental toughness plays a major role.

For example, I love Chili's restaurant. My wife and I have been eating there for thirty years. Every birthday, anniversary, or celebration seems to take place at Chili's. My friends have made fun of me for years about this, but I really like it. The habit I've formed at Chili's is ordering the chips and dip every time we're there. When I was younger and chasing tennis balls all day, it never posed a problem. Now that I'm older and off the court, I gain weight just looking at chips and dip. So every time I see a Chili's Restaurant, my emotions move to good feelings, and the next thing I think about are chips. This is classical conditioning, and I'm like one of Pavlov's dogs. In order to become a fat loser, I had to override my emotional desire with logical thinking, telling myself that chips make me fat. And it worked, as long as I didn't allow emotions into my decision-making process. We've all done this throughout our lives, most likely at an unconscious level. We override our feelings and use logic to serve our best interests. I'm simply suggesting you become more acutely aware of this process to move to the next level. Emotion will motivate you and logic will keep you on track. The combination of these two forces used properly will propel you more quickly than anything else.

"Use emotion to motivate and logic to steer."

Critical Thinking Question

ANALYZE THE LAST TIME YOU CHEATED ON YOUR DIET. WAS IT LOGICAL OR EMOTIONAL THINKING THAT MOTIVATED YOU?

Action Step

Every time you think about your diet in the next seven days, ask yourself whether it's a logical or emotional thought. This process will help you identify and separate the two.

MENTAL-TOUGHNESS STRATEGY #57

STOP EGO-BASED THINKING

One of the greatest challenges we've encountered over the years in our fat-loser program is the shame new dieters feel about dieting. I'm not talking about feeling shame for being fat; I'm talking about feeling shame for *dieting*. This idea surprised me. The pervasiveness of the message that *"diets don't work"* has created a mindset among fat people, leading them to hide the truth about dieting and sometimes to lie about it. The idea that diets don't work is nonsense, but that's beside the point. Dieting is a disciplined and measured method of consuming food. In other words, dieters are conscious of the food they eat and are strategic about their choices. Fat people unconsciously eat all foods in front of them with no strategy in mind. Which group is following a more intelligent course of action?

My suggestion is to move your ego out of the way and ignore the messages of the masses. Seventy percent of the population is fat, so why would you listen to them about weight loss? Every fat loser reaches a point in the process where they must decide to go forward or give up. During the *excitement* stage of dieting, this decision isn't a problem. All you can think about is how good you're going to look and feel when you reach your goal. But then you hit the next stage, the *season of pain*, when the excitement is gone. It's the stage in which you're tired of having to discipline yourself and you miss your favorite foods. This is the time when it's easy to fall prey to the mass consciousness saying diets don't work and you should quit.

It's important to remember that while the masses are smart, educated, and capable, they typically don't fulfill their goals. Listening to them is a liability you can't afford if you want to be fit. When it comes to the message of the medical community claiming obesity is a disease, think independently. Doctors are following this practice so they can bill insurance companies when they talk to patients about losing weight. If you follow the money, it will usually lead to the motivation. Dieting is a discipline to be proud of and not something to suffer through secretly while simultaneously denying it. So check your ego at the door and never allow it to impede your progress. Let the masses denounce dieting while you build the body of your dreams.

"There's no place for ego-based thinking in becoming a fat loser. Select your diet, follow your plan, and ignore the message of the masses."

Critical Thinking Question

ARE YOU LETTING YOUR EGO CLOUD YOUR THINKING ABOUT DIETING?

Action Step

Take pride in the fact that you have the discipline to diet your way to fitness.

MENTAL-TOUGHNESS STRATEGY #58

GO TO WAR

Fat is not a toy with which to play. Fat is the enemy you decimate, and as quickly as possible. This is not a game or a hobby; this is a *war*. Being fat will make you sick and possibly kill you. Not something to be taken lightly but something to annihilate. The diet commercials flooding the airwaves promise you can eat all you want while the weight just dissolves. People believe it, until they fail. Selling the idea that dieting is easy is nothing new, and it's made many companies wealthy beyond their wildest dreams. It's simply not true. The problem isn't with the foods these companies manufacture; the mindset they sell does the damage. Telling a fat person that becoming fit is going to be easy is a crime.

It's like doctors telling you a shot won't hurt. As soon as they insert the needle you jump out of your skin because you weren't expecting the pain. That's the reason most doctors say the shot is going to sting in order to prepare you for the pain. Then when they insert the needle, it's not a surprise, and you think *that wasn't too bad*. It's all about creating expectation and mental preparation. That's the reason I'm suggesting you prepare yourself by seeing your diet as a battle that pits your old eating habits against the new ones, and the first time you become hungry and crave your favorite foods, you'll feel the strength of the old habits. They have been deeply ingrained for years and won't submit without a fight. Your new habits hope to replace the old ones, but they're up against a formidable force. Thirty consecutive days of forcing the new habits into your life will begin to weaken the old ones. If you cheat on your diet, they'll roar back and wipe out your new habits. Critical thinking dictates that you aggressively approach becoming a fat loser and recognize it for the war it is so you won't be shocked or surprised when the going gets tough.

"Dieting is a war between old habits and new ones.

It's you against you, and the you

that wants it most will win."

---

of emotional creatures who allow other people to think for them. This probably won't change in our lifetime, but that doesn't mean we have to fall into this societal trap. So keep it simple, stay on your diet, become fit, and be proud that you're strong enough to go against the grain and think for yourself.

"Fat people are ashamed of dieting. Fat losers think for themselves and proudly proclaim they're declaring war on their poor eating habits."

Critical Thinking Question

ON A SCALE OF 1-7, 7 AS THE MOST OFTEN, HOW OFTEN DO YOU THINK FOR YOURSELF?

Action Step

Visit www.FatLosers.com and enroll in the FREE twenty-one-day video-training course.

MENTAL-TOUGHNESS STRATEGY #60

BE A ROLE MODEL

Seventy percent of adult Americans are overweight or obese. Thirty-three percent of American children are overweight or obese. The Center for Disease Control in Atlanta states that by 2027, ninety percent of Americans will be overweight or obese. The statistics are staggering and growing worse every day. The obesity epidemic is on track to becoming the greatest health issue in American history. That's the bad news. The good news is that very soon, *you'll* no longer be part of it. In a country where most people are fat, fit people are quickly becoming role models. Like it or not, fat people are watching you. Your battle and subsequent victory will be a source of inspiration for an untold number of people in your life.

Two ways are available to handle this newfound status: you can reject or embrace it. I'm suggesting you embrace it, but not out of any sense of altruism or obligation. Being a role model serves as an additional emotional motivator to keep you on track. Becoming a fat loser is only the first step. *Remaining* a fat loser is the real challenge, and recidivism rates in weight loss are extremely high. So a fat loser *remaining* a fat loser is an anomaly and means you have the opportunity to become a role model. In mental toughness, we look to emotion to fuel and sustain motivation, and being a role model people want to emulate may provide an enhanced level of emotional motivation. It's comforting to have people who want to be like you, and if you're fit, that will happen. Use it to your advantage and help others along the way. It's a win-win scenario.

"Fat people are judged and discriminated against in society. Fat losers are celebrated."

Critical Thinking Question

ARE YOU READY TO BE A ROLE MODEL?

Action Step

Pick five famous fat people and ask your friends and family members to tell you their first impressions of them? Ninety percent of the time people will reply, "He or she is fat."

MENTAL-TOUGHNESS STRATEGY #61

BE POSITIVE

Positive thinking is overused, overrated, and emotionally driven, often ignoring contrary evidence. But positive thinking proves to be more productive than negative thinking in most situations, including weight loss. The ability to maintain a positive attitude throughout the process increases the probability that you'll stay on the diet and succeed. Positive thinking provides an additional dose of motivation as well as helping to minimize the suffering accompanying a major habit-change. Be positive about everything in this process, not as a philosophy, but as a Mental-Toughness Strategy. Use positive self-talk and develop the habit of using uplifting language with yourself and others. Instead of describing your struggle to stay on the diet, express your excitement about being on the path to becoming a fat loser.

Tell people about how good it feels to become more fit and healthy every day, and how happy you are to be moving into the future with new and empowering eating habits. Talk about the invigoration of your exercise regimen and the feeling of satisfaction afterwards. Share with people how inspiring it is to work out at the health club among all those fit and sexy people. Keep in mind that it doesn't matter if you initially feel this way or not. If you consistently say positive things to yourself and others, you'll begin to believe them and it will push you toward greater success. Being positive around other people isn't for their benefit, it's for yours. Because positive thinking is driven by emotion and doesn't rely on evidence, reason, or facts, it's effectively a form of self-induced mental programming that persuades the subconscious mind that your words are true. If you allow it, using positive language will impact your conscious mind as well. If you were making a business decision, I'd tell you to avoid positive thinking because it's emotionally driven and clouds judgment. In weight loss, however, it works wonders.

"Fat people see diets negatively. Fat losers see diets positively because they serve their best interests."

Critical Thinking Question

ON A SCALE OF 1-7, 7 AS THE MOST OFTEN, HOW OFTEN DO YOU INCORPORATE POSITIVE THINKING INTO YOUR QUEST TO BECOME A FAT LOSER?

Action Step

To learn the language that world-class performers use with themselves and others, read *What to Say When You Talk to Yourself*, by Dr. Shad Helmstetter

MENTAL-TOUGHNESS STRATEGY #62

EMBRACE MOMENTUM

The first weeks of breaking old eating habits can be a shock to your system. Some of these habits may have developed as early as childhood and are deeply ingrained. That's the reason to build momentum as quickly as possible and embrace every aspect of it.

We all know the power of physical momentum, a wave gaining power in the ocean with every swell; a train leaving the station and gaining speed; a runner hitting perfect stride. Psychological momentum is less understood yet just as powerful. Athletes believing they can win, business people making their first million, and fat people losing three pounds the first week are examples of precursors to psychological momentum. To embrace this magnificent force of nature, lose as much weight in the first few weeks of your diet as possible. Nothing creates momentum faster than early success. The more momentum you build the easier it becomes to lose weight. Embracing momentum means talking about it to yourself and others, and being acutely aware of the way it feels as well how it affects you. It's an exciting process, and the more you embrace it the stronger it grows.

Celebrate every part of your success in the dieting process, from pounds and inches lost to energy and vitality gained. The positive emotion you experience from these early successes will fuel the wave of momentum and motivate you to continue moving in the right direction. A dieter engaged in full-blown momentum is one of the most exciting images I've ever witnessed or experienced.

Momentum is not only about losing weight, but also about life. It's about beginning to believe you're a powerful, self-reliant individual capable of achieving any goal. You can expect momentum to occur at some point, and you should embrace it whole-heartedly. Psychological momentum will reduce the suffering you experience and expedite your success, and it may just change every aspect of your life for the better.

"Fat people slog slowly through diets, continually stopping and starting. Fat losers move quickly and continue building momentum until they reach their goals."

Critical Thinking Question

ON A SCALE OF 1-7, 7 AS THE MOST, HOW MUCH MOMENTUM DO YOU HAVE ON YOUR CURRENT DIET?

Action Step

Identify times in your life when you experienced great psychological momentum, and take the same steps on your diet to re-create it.

MENTAL-TOUGHNESS STRATEGY #63

BUILD A TEAM

In 2000, overweight and struggling, my first step was seeing my doctor. When it comes to having the things you want, you can either go it alone or call on experts to guide you. I recommend the latter. I told my doctor I thought I needed to drop the extra twenty pounds I was carrying around. He said, "How about forty?" I was a little shocked when he said, "Steve, you write and speak about mental toughness and critical thinking all over the world, so here's a dose of your own material: you're deluding yourself. You're forty pounds overweight. What are you going to do about it?" You gotta love it when people use your own words against you. I say that jokingly because it was the best advice he could've given me.

I wish more doctors had the courage to tell their patients the truth. Sadly, many doctors are terrified of losing patients, so they ignore the subject of weight loss completely. After my doctor's visit, I booked an appointment with a local weight-loss expert and we put a plan together. After that, I went home to my wife, told her my plan, and asked for her support emotionally and physically in tossing the junk food in the garbage and cooking more healthful meals. Then I went to the gym and talked to a trainer about a workout to lose the weight. Next, I spent three hours writing down my eating and exercising schedule for the next twelve weeks so I'd be completely prepared and organized. And the last thing I did was construct a vision board by cutting out pictures in fitness magazines of bodies I wanted to emulate and taping them to a poster board. The next day I officially launched my diet and went to work.

Twelve weeks later the weight was gone and I felt like a million bucks. Now, as heroic as the story sounds, it's really much messier in reality. Along the road to going from a fat person to a fat loser, I experienced the pain of cravings, frustration of plateaus, and the self-pity of denying myself the pleasure of my favorite foods. Keeping me on track was the team of experts and support people I'd assembled before I embarked on the journey. You can lose weight on your own and succeed, but why not leverage the expertise and support of people interested in your success? Why make it harder than it needs to be? Suffering for suffering's sake is foolish. Build a team before you begin and see how powerful it can be. You wouldn't go to war without a team, so why would you fight an important personal battle without one?

"Fat people silently suffer and singularly struggle. Fat losers minimize their suffering and struggle through the support and assistance of others."

Critical Thinking Question

HAVE YOU ASSEMBLED A TEAM TO SUPPORT YOU THROUGH THIS PROCESS?

Action Step

Assemble a team of experts and support people in the following areas: overall health, diet, exercise, meal planning, support, and motivation.

MENTAL-TOUGHNESS STRATEGY #64

EMBRACE CHANGE

All of us want to achieve better results without having to change. Everyone wants to go to heaven but no one wants to die. This folly is human nature. At best, it's delusional thinking. At worst, it's insanity. The thinking that made you fat won't make you thin and the eating habits that bloated your body must be eliminated. There is no easy way out. The very essence of the weight-loss-fitness process revolves around major habit- transformation. The old disempowering eating habits are like indestructible steel cables that bind us and keep us fat. It's easy to say, "Just change," but in reality it's a difficult obstacle to overcome. Old habits are not fond of human meddling, and they will do everything possible to dissuade you from replacing them. One of the strongest habits I had to change was eating ice cream; specifically hot fudge sundaes and butter scotch milk shakes. I averaged at least two a week, and the cravings I experienced when in the process of breaking the habit were extremely strong. My candy bar habit didn't go down without a fight, either.

I found the craftiness of these habits bizarre when you try to break them. Things go through your mind, such as "I'll only have one" or "No one will know." It's as if an evil alien resides in our minds, trying to save the old habits at any cost. During the early days of my struggle, I resisted the habit-change and even whined silently about my dislike. Eventually I learned to embrace the change instead of resisting it, and that acceptance made the process much easier. The struggle for habit-change lies in your best interest, so why not embrace the change, and welcome the new eating and exercising habits? Become excited about these positive, life-affirming, and healthful changes. Once the habit-change-battle ends, all you'll have to do is guard the door carefully to be sure the old habits don't return. And you can be assured, they will try. But it's easier to protect a new habit after it's in place than it is to put it into place. The good news is the war won't last long and the benefits will be worth it. Embrace the exciting changes and you'll make the journey more comfortable and satisfactory.

> *"Think positively about changing your eating habits because affirmation makes it easier. Think critically about changing your eating habits because it will make you healthier."*

Critical Thinking Question

IN PAST EXPERIENCES WITH DIETS, HAVE YOU RESISTED OR EMBRACED THE NECESSARY HABIT-CHANGES?

Action Step

Just for today, have a positive attitude about changing your eating habits and see if the process becomes easier.

MENTAL-TOUGHNESS STRATEGY #65

USE FAILURE AS FUEL

Everyone I know has failed on a diet, including me. I'll bet everyone you know has, too. Diets and failure seem synonymous for a reason: habit-change is difficult to achieve. The more addicted you are to a habit, the harder it is to change. Habit-change is like swimming upstream, and most people simply tire of fighting the current. It's much easier and more comfortable just to let yourself float gently down the river of life. Sadly, most people adopt this approach, not only in weight loss, but also in their daily lives.

Fighting the good fight requires diligent effort, and the potential for failure is high when it comes to changing ingrained habits of twenty, thirty, or forty years. As a matter of fact, a habit *that old* is not a habit, it's an *institution*. The bottom line is while we've all failed at diets, failure should be used as a source of motivation. Most people fail a few times and quit, but fat losers use failure as fuel to persist until they succeed. It's one of the most closely-held and well-guarded secrets of great performers, probably because they're not proud of it. I've used it my whole life and I *am* proud of it. I'll give you my most extreme example: When I finished college, I got married and started a new business. We had little money to pay bills while we grew the business, so I took a job at a gas station working the graveyard shift from eleven at night until seven in the morning. It only paid five dollars an hour, but combined with my wife's waitressing job, it was enough to squeak by.

We didn't sleep much in those days, but at least we were in business. As the weeks of running on fumes financially and emotionally turned into months, the fund-raising business we'd started out of our bedroom closet was failing. We just couldn't seem to get it off the ground. I was really exhausted one day and feeling down when I pulled into the parking lot of my cousin's multi-million-dollar company. He'd inherited it from my uncle, and it made him a rich man. I climbed out of my car at the same time as my cousin, and he said, "I hear you're pumping gas for a living, Steve. Way to go." Then he laughed and climbed back into his new Cadillac. His sarcasm happened more than thirty years ago and I can still feel it burn. Little did I know that his five-second insult would motivate me to become a millionaire. Every time I'd become tired, depressed, or discouraged, I used his words to turn into *Superman*. I'm sure my cousin doesn't remember that day, but it turned out to be a gift. The point of my story reminds me that failure is powerful when turned inside out. Use it to fuel your fire and it will empower you.

"The masses use failure as an excuse to quit.

The great ones use failure as fuel to succeed."

Critical Thinking Question

WHAT HIGHLY EMOTIONAL FAILURES HAVE YOU EXPERIENCED THAT COULD BE REINTERPRETED AND USED TO DRIVE YOUR DIET-SUCCESS?

Action Step

Identify your five greatest failures and pick the most powerful one to fuel your weight loss.

MENTAL-TOUGHNESS STRATEGY #66

EXPECT EXTRA BENEFITS

I lost weight because I was embarrassed that friends I hadn't seen in years didn't recognize me. I was also having trouble breathing during workouts, and it scared me. I figured it would feel good to be fit again, and it did. I didn't know that losing extra weight would produce derivative benefits. It was a pleasant surprise. For instance, my sex life improved. Just feeling good about my body was the beginning, but being fit made me want to have more sex. My confidence in business improved. Taking control of a situation out of control gave me newfound feelings of competence. In short, I felt like I could do anything. My financial life also improved. My new body offered me energy I hadn't had in years and a level of creativity I'd never experienced.

My marriage improved because I felt better about myself and our relationship. I became a more patient, loving partner. My workouts improved, thanks to a new level of stamina and actually seeing results in the mirror. It's difficult to admire your abs with forty pounds of flab on them. My attitude improved because I found myself excited about life again. I felt as though now that I was fit, I was moving forward instead of struggling to survive. My overall sense of well-being was also greatly enhanced by becoming fit. There's something comforting and self-affirming about solving your own problems through self-discipline and mental toughness. It really inspired me. These are only a few examples of the additional benefits and positive consequences of becoming a fat loser. Think about these things when the going gets tough and it will help you realize that the pain and struggle you're experiencing is worth it. Once you become fit, you're life will never be the same. Isn't that exciting? Pay the price once and reap the benefits permanently. You gotta love that!

"Fat people don't know the benefits they're missing. Fat losers see the vast rewards awaiting them. The more fit they become, the more rewards they reap."

Critical Thinking Question

ARE YOU REALLY AWARE OF ALL THE BENEFITS OF BEING FIT?

Action Step

Make a list of the ten most meaningful benefits you'll reap as a result of becoming fit, and read the list every time you feel hungry.

MENTAL-TOUGHNESS STRATEGY #67

GET ORGANIZED

There's an old saying you've probably heard: "everyone wants to win, but few people are willing to prepare to win." Fighting fat is a war that requires serious preparation. You must prepare by selecting a diet and exercise program. You should build a team of people to support you along the way. And last but not least, you should prepare yourself for the marathon mentality it requires to go the distance despite the pain. All of these actions are crucial to your success, and they all require organization, both physical and mental. Before I became serious about becoming a fat loser, I ignored this advice and paid the price, and I knew better.

Years ago I asked Martina Navratilova, the number-one female tennis player in the world at the time and by far the most fit, how she maintained her fitness on the road. She told me, "You have to be organized and prepare your meals in advance so you don't make eating-decisions when you're hungry. I always travel with a cooler packed with my meals." Martina spoke these words twenty-five years ago and I still remember them today, but I'd ignored her advice on my first few diets and failed. I made good eating-decisions when I was full and lousy ones when I was hungry, the very thing about which she warned me.

I finally decided to take Martina's advice and get organized. I planned every meal and workout in advance. I prepared to stay on my diet at social functions, speaking events, on holidays, and at any place brimming with junk food. And it worked. Your willingness to organize your life around your diet is directly proportional to your belief in your ability to succeed. Becoming organized is easy but requires an investment of time and energy. There's no glory in it. It's banal and boring. It's also necessary for success. You wouldn't wage a war without preparing every detail within your control, knowing that once the first bullet is fired, many variables will be *out* of your control. The more preparation you do in advance, the more you can focus on the new challenges for which you couldn't have prepared. Luckily, no actual bullets will be fired in this war of weight loss, but make no mistake about it: this battle *is* a war. It's a war of the old and new habits and a battle you must win. So be certain you're organized before launching your attack.

"Fat losers prepare to win the war of weight loss on every front. Every detail is planned in advance, and every potential threat is assessed."

Critical Thinking Question

ARE YOU PHYSICALLY, MENTALLY, AND EMOTIONALLY PREPARED TO WAGE WAR WITH YOUR OLD HABITS?

Action Step

Get organized in every aspect of the dieting process before you begin.

MENTAL-TOUGHNESS STRATEGY #68

EXPECT PEACE OF MIND

To suggest you to go to war and expect peace of mind may seem counterintuitive. But a sense of calmness prevails from being prepared to perform, and it's rooted in the mindset that recognizes you've done all you can to succeed. No mental energy is wasted on fear, regret, or intimidation. All thoughts are laser-focused on the successful execution of your plan. In a war of habits in which the outcome is determined by your ability to follow a diet and exercise regimen, the only variable in the equation is *mental toughness*. Once you know you're going to direct one hundred percent of your mental energy toward this process, the battle is effectively over before it begins. This energy creates peace of mind that few dieters' experience.

Mental toughness, professional preparation, and the expertise as well as the support of others can turn a struggle into a peaceful, calm, loving adventure. Let me be clear, I'm not saying that achieving this elevated state of mind in the midst of war is easy; I'm only suggesting that it's *possible and preferable*. Expecting to achieve it moves you closer to manifestation. The psychological benefits of waging a war with a calm, calculated, consciousness cannot be overstated. Not only does this mindset make it easier but also frees you from the emotional mood swings that cloud judgment and lead to poor decision-making. Making major changes in your eating, exercise, and social patterns is stressful enough without adding a stressed mindset to the equation. Once I decided to become a fat loser, I immediately felt a sense of well-being and peace of mind regarding my health that I'd never experienced before. I knew what I had to do, and I knew that I would do it. My success was simply a matter of time, and those calming thoughts eased my struggle. You can do the same.

"Fat losers don't slow down, they calm down. They know the battle of the bulge is fought more intelligently with a peaceful mindset."

Critical Thinking Question

ARE YOU EXPECTING TO EXPERIENCE STRESS OR PEACE OF MIND ON YOUR FAT-LOSER JOURNEY?

Action Step

Make a list of the things that will help you create a sense of calm and peace of mind in the midst of your weight-loss war.

MENTAL-TOUGHNESS STRATEGY #69

EMBRACE PERSISTENCE

Persistence is to weight loss what carbon is to steel. It's essential. No one escapes the pain of the process. Having never taken dieting seriously, I was shocked to find that it was more difficult than I expected. I started out overconfident but was quickly humbled when I was tempted to quit. I began negotiating with myself to cheat a little here and there, until I woke up and realized this was the way I got fat in the first place. It's embarrassing for me to admit this temptation as a mental-toughness coach to some of the world's largest companies. Shouldn't I have known better? Shouldn't I have taken my own advice? Of course, and that's the way I end up with a bloated body. Not only should personal-development authors read their own books but also heed their own advice. Even when I got serious, I still expected it to be *easier*. The truth is it took twelve weeks of persistence to reach my goal.

For some of you with more weight to lose, it will take longer. Twelve weeks will only be a warm-up for you. No matter where you begin or want to go, be mentally prepared to persist when you want to quit, cheat, or slack off. There are no cease-fires in this war. It's twenty-four-seven, and the goal means decimating your opponent as quickly and efficiently as possible while sustaining the fewest number of casualties. Like any war, a battle between habits is exciting at first but quickly descends into a daily slog through the mess of multiple factors, including hunger, cravings, change, and on-going temptation. In other words, the process grows old, fast. The beginning stage is exciting and full of hope for a brighter future, and the ending stage is thrilling because you can see the finish line. The challenging part is the middle stage, or what fat losers call, *the season of pain*. The excitement has faded and the outcome is still in question. It's only you and your habits slugging it out in dog-fight fashion vying for the prize. This is the time when persistence will make or break you. The diet will do the work as long as you're strong and persistent enough to stay on it. So prepare yourself to be more persistent than you may ever have been by deciding you'll do whatever it takes to win. This philosophy alone will guarantee your success.

"Victory goes to the strong and persistent performer who refuses to quit. There's no secret to success. Work and keep working until you win."

Critical Thinking Question

ON A SCALE OF 1-7, 7 AS THE MOST PERSISTENT, HOW PERSISTENT HAVE YOU BEEN ON PREVIOUS DIETS?

Action Step

Decide to persist on your diet until you succeed. The pain won't last forever, and the closer you move to success the easier it will become.

MENTAL-TOUGHNESS STRATEGY #70

PAY THE PRICE

When I was working for one of the wealthiest weight loss companies on wall street, the greatest roadblocks were clients wanting to negotiate the price of their weight loss. People loved the diet. The food was tasty, the delivery system was well organized, and the psychological training was effective. Technically speaking, there were no issues. Emotionally speaking, however, every client was eager to challenge the system and figure out a way to cut corners. While I'm in favor of reducing the pain of the process, weight-loss systems are designed to be followed to the letter, and sometimes even the slightest deviation will throw the physiological formula into disarray. This is the place in which critical thinking plays a huge part. The delusion leads you to believe you can succeed with a system you don't follow. This belief is emotionally-fueled thinking that ignores logic while expecting positive results. Critical thinking demands that emotion be removed from the equation and the system be followed in order to work.

We all know everything in life has a price, and the bigger the benefit the more it costs. If you want a successful relationship with your spouse or significant other, there is a price to pay. If you want to be financially independent, there is a price to pay. And if you want to be physically fit, there is a price to pay. No one gets a free ride, and no one negotiates there way out of doing the work and enduring the pain. Whether you're a spouse raising kids or a movie star preparing for a role, you'll pay the price or you will fail. The choice is yours and time will tell. Everyone talks a good game, but few people follow through to conclusion.

You're the only one who can make the decision to pay the price. It's your body and your battle to fight. No one can do it for you. The only variable in this equation is that everyone's price is different, so when you agree to pay it, you're effectively signing a blank check. For some people, success will come quickly. Others will endure a long, drawn-out battle. Whichever experience you encounter, you'll have to pay the price in full and in advance. After coaching thousands of people through the process, I can assure you the results are worth it. Whatever price you pay will be a pittance compared to the benefits you receive.

"You're already paying the price for being overweight, and if you stay fat, you'll be paying for the rest of your life. Pay the price one time to become a fat loser and reap the rewards permanently."

Critical Thinking Question

ARE YOU MENTALLY AND EMOTIONALLY PREPARED TO PAY A PRICE FOR WEIGHT LOSS THAT HAS YET TO BE DETERMINED?

Action Step

Take your psychological pulse by assigning yourself a rating on a scale of 1-7. Seven means you'll pay any price to succeed. Where do you rate on the scale?

MENTAL-TOUGHNESS STRATEGY #71

FOCUS ON RESULTS

I failed at my first few attempts at dieting because I was focused on the food instead of the results. Like most people, I spent a great deal of time thinking about the foods I was missing and wallowing in self-pity for having to wean myself off them. Fat losers focus on the results they're achieving from day one of their diet and this attitude keeps them moving forward with excitement and enthusiasm. Weighing yourself every day is one way of realizing this attitude. Carefully tracking your body measurements is another. The focal point of your mental energy can only center on one thing at a time, and keeping it focused on results crowds out thoughts of food, hunger, and cravings.

When I discovered this fact the diet became easier to follow. Looking in the proverbial rearview mirror doesn't serve anyone's best interest, so I began looking at my present results while dreaming of the future. This view did wonders for my attitude and pulled me out of the emotional doldrums about missing my old junk-food diet. The beautiful thing is as soon as you begin to see the slightest bit of success, the process becomes easier. To suffer when you're succeeding is one thing, but quite another when you have no forward momentum. The good news is that many healthful diets offer solid results in a short time. The key lies in being able to stay focused on the results before you actually realize them. I did it by hanging a vision board in my home gym where I spend an hour every day. That reinforcement encouraged me for the first few weeks before I'd experienced any serious results. Today, with the advent of cellular cleansing, you can start losing weight within twenty-four hours, which is extremely motivating. Technology has made becoming fit easier to achieve. So develop the habit of monitoring your mental energy and its direction. The process will move more quickly and be more enjoyable.

"Fat people focus on the foods they're missing.

Fat losers focus on achieving results."

Critical Thinking Question

DURING THE COURSE OF AN AVERAGE DAY, WHAT PERCENTAGE OF YOUR MENTAL ENERGY IS DIRECTED TOWARD YOUR WEIGHT-LOSS RESULTS?

Action Step

List three ways to keep your focus on results during the difficult days of dieting.

MENTAL-TOUGHNESS STRATEGY #72

BECOME MENTALLY TOUGH

If you're going to become a fat loser, you'll have to get tough. Not tough like John Wayne, but tough on *yourself*. The days of making excuses are over, and now it's just you and your diet. Don't fool yourself into believing because you selected a diet, became organized, and prepared for success that you won't experience physical, emotional, and mental challenges. You will. Everyone does. The secret lies in embracing this reality and telling yourself you're strong enough to succeed. Tennis taught me this secret in the 1970s. I'd be battling with a competitor, physically and mentally exhausted after playing for three hours, and the score was four-to-four or five-to-five in the third set. At that point, I was no longer excited about the match, I merely wanted to win and leave the court. Unfortunately, it's not that easy. Great competitors won't let up even under the most extreme conditions. These athletes have been trained to fight, and wouldn't know the way to let up if you told them.

There's only one-way to win these brutal matches, and that's to get tough and meet your opponent head-on. No tricks, games, or gimmicks, just a face-to-face battle whereby the tougher player prevails. Nothing is pretty or impressive about becoming tough. It's only a decision you make if you want to win. Dieting is the same. At some point in the process, you realize you merely have to swallow your pride and get tough if you're going to succeed. This is more of a realization than a strategy, yet the process of recognizing it is a strategy in itself. The specifics of becoming tough are simple: you have to be strong enough to stick to your diet when you're hungry, craving unhealthful foods, or bored with the foods you're eating. My technique is straightforward: I look at the foods that made me fat and say, "I'm bigger than you. You cannot defeat me." My desire to become fit is greater than the urge to eat junk food. At the end of the day, getting tough is a choice, and it's choice we must make in order to succeed.

"Fat losers learn to become mentally tough and break the chains binding them to unhealthful habits."

Critical Thinking Question

ON A SCALE OF 1-7, 7 AS THE TOUGHEST, HOW TOUGH ARE YOU ON YOURSELF WHEN IT COMES TO YOUR DIET?"

Action Step

Make a list of five ways you can increase your level of mental toughness.

MENTAL-TOUGHNESS STRATEGY #73

BUILD SELF-ESTEEM

Few subjects are so misunderstood as self-esteem, but the definition is actually quite simple: self-esteem is the reputation we have with ourselves. This view becomes critical not only to our sense of well-being and happiness in life, but also to our level of confidence when we're approaching a goal like weight loss. In my two-year study of 500 fat and 500 fit people, one of the most common complaints fat people cited was having so little faith in their ability to stay on the diet. Add this to fat people's feelings of inferiority plus shame and you have a recipe for disaster. Of course fit people experience these same phenomena, but with opposite results. They use the confidence gained from their weight-loss success as the engine to power new successes in others areas of life.

The million-dollar question is how do you generate the confidence to lose weight when you've never succeeded before or you've succeeded but gained it all back? Many people I interviewed attempted to convince themselves that this time would be different, and while it's a noble and honest strategy, it didn't work for most of the people I interviewed. The better answer is to borrow it. In other words, borrow the self-esteem and confidence from someone with the power to convince you that you can do it. Confidence borrowing and lending consists of temporarily transferring one person's belief to another in the interest of performance. For example, would George W. Bush have been as decisive after 9/11 without Vice President Cheney? Love or hate him, Cheney is about as confident and self-assured a man as I've ever encountered. Bush borrowed Cheney's confidence and used it to his advantage. Hollywood legend has it that the great comedian George Burns wouldn't have been as successful without his wife and professional sidekick, Gracie Allen. Burns borrowed Allen's confidence. I'm sure you can recall a personal experience in which you did the same thing, and this strategy can be applied to weight loss as well. You need only borrow confidence until you start achieving results. Once this happens, you'll have the confidence you need to move to the next level and restore your own reputation with yourself.

"Fat people with low self-esteem use it as an excuse for quitting. Fat losers with low self-esteem borrow confidence from someone stronger until they're strong enough to succeed on their own."

Critical Thinking Question

ON A SCALE OF 1-7, 7 AS THE HIGHEST, RATE YOUR LEVEL OF SELF-ESTEEM.

Action Step

If you need to borrow confidence from someone else, make a list of potential candidates. This group might include a personal trainer, spouse, or life coach, anyone believing in you long enough for you to achieve results and regain your confidence.

MENTAL-TOUGHNESS STRATEGY #74

MONITOR YOUR VIBRATION

A person's rate of vibration is the blend of physical, mental, and emotional energy they emit in communication. It's an interesting phenomenon because people can say something verbally while their vibrations indicate the opposite. We've all experienced this vibration ourselves. We've even done this *to* ourselves by saying one thing while believing another. This cognitive dissonance leads our vibration to abandon us and reflect our true belief. When I failed on my first two diets, I told myself I wanted to lose weight, yet I wasn't truly committed to the process. Mentally I wanted to lose weight, but emotionally I wasn't certain I was willing to pay the price. This psychological disconnect could be heard in my voice and seen in my body language, and generated an inconsistent performance. As a result, I exhibited the classic approach-avoid performance trap whereby I moved toward a goal and then moved away from it. It's similar to taking one step forward and two steps back, and it's the direct result of conflicting thoughts. This conflict led to my ultimate failure. The solution is using self-talk to program yourself for success and a serious commitment to staying on your diet and losing the weight. This combination will create a harmonious vibration that will keep you moving forward without looking back. Once I discovered this solution, I started telling myself I was moving closer to my goal everyday and nothing could stop me. I'd say things such as, "I'm a healthy eating machine that can't be stopped" and "Fitness is my priority. Food is not."

If you've never used self-talk programming before, it may seem silly at first, but I assure you it's not. Human beings are programmed from birth to death with messages from people of influence, the media, society, religion, school, and other sources. Some programming is worthwhile and some is not. The greatest source of programming, however, comes from the words we say to ourselves all day long, everyday, over the course of a lifetime. For most of us it's random, but the most intelligent performers construct the language they use with themselves carefully because they understand its power. When you begin talking to yourself in positive ways about diet and exercise, your rate of vibration reflects your thoughts and creates congruency. When I followed this method on my last diet, I felt incredibly empowered, and it made the process much easier. This is the power of the mind over the body, and it's easy to use once you understand it.

"Fat people approach dieting half-heartedly. Fit people approach dieting with a do-or-die commitment, and this intensity vibrates through every fiber of their beings."

Critical Thinking Question

ON A SCALE OF 1-7, 7 AS THE HIGHEST, HOW HIGH IS YOUR RATE OF VIBRATION AS IT RELATES TO DIETING?

Action Step

Begin to monitor your self-talk and rate of vibration.

MENTAL-TOUGHNESS STRATEGY #75

REWARD EXECUTION

Two types of goal-setting systems are available. One rewards you for results and the other for execution. I've researched them both for more than thirty years through case studies, surveys, and corporate clients worldwide. On the surface it seems naïve not to select the rewards-for-results approach. After all, aren't results the bottom line? Of course they are, and to deny it is foolhardy. With human beings, however, other factors need to be considered, such as the psychological fulfillment of hitting benchmarks en route to the ultimate goal. The emotional satisfaction of staying on the diet in the early stages and seeing the first substantial weight loss is positive reinforcement. The excitement of experiencing psychological momentum begins to build and makes the process easier. These important markers along the way should be recognized and rewarded. That's the reason I've found execution-based goal-setting to be the most effective overall.

The key is to reward yourself for successfully executing the major steps in your strategy. For example, let's say your goal is losing fifty pounds. Your plan calls for twenty-four weeks of one hundred percent compliance on the diet plus exercising five days a week. You could wait to reward yourself after you lose the fifty pounds or you could reward yourself every seven days for staying on the diet. Which system would be more motivating? Success in anything is based on execution, and execution should be rewarded. I prefer to offer small nonfood rewards to keep people on track and moving forward. The big reward comes when the overall goal is achieved. These strategies worked in my research and personal experience, but experiment and find the type that works for you.

As long as you achieve the goal and become a fat loser, the method of arrival at this goal is secondary. Execution-based goal setting seems to minimize the pain for many people while keeping them sufficiently motivated to continue fighting.

No matter which system you use, never apply food as a reward for weight loss or exercise success. I know this reward is popular, and it's the reason so many people fail on their diets or regain the weight. Using unhealthful food as a reward for building healthful habits is counterproductive. It's like rewarding an alcoholic for staying sober by giving him an alcoholic drink. Use healthful, positive, life-affirming nonfood rewards to create congruency as you're losing weight to improve your life. One of my favorite rewards is buying a massage after hitting a benchmark. Another is taking a guitar lesson. These positive rewards keep me on track. Think of some reward that fits your life and keeps you moving toward your goal. Map out your long-term weight-loss strategy, including critical benchmarks along the way. If it's a six-month goal, what will you weigh at the end of each month and what reward will you give yourself when you reach it? You'll find this execution-based reward system more enjoyable and easier to follow.

"Fat people make excuses for being overweight.

Fat losers focus on executing the solution

instead of making excuses for the problem."

Critical Thinking Question

ARE YOU WAITING TOO LONG TO REWARD YOURSELF IN THE WEIGHT-LOSS PROCESS?

Action Step

List five nonfood rewards you can give yourself when you arrive at various milestones on your weight-loss journey.

MENTAL-TOUGHNESS STRATEGY #76

EMBRACE RECOGNITION

Weight-loss success draws attention and recognition every place you go. In a country where seventy percent of the population is overweight or obese, your success is a minority condition and you need to be ready for an overwhelming, disproportionate level of recognition. My suggestion is not to push it away or deny your success as a form of modesty, but to embrace it fully and bask in the glory of a battle well fought and won. By embracing the kudos and compliments you receive about your weight loss, you accept the fact that you accomplished this feat through your own self-discipline and deserve recognition for your success. Denying people's compliments doesn't make you modest, it only makes it seem as though you got lucky or sick and somehow the weight just fell off. This impression doesn't foster additional motivation to maintain your success, and it almost implies that you're *ashamed* of it. I'm not asking you to embrace the recognition you'll receive to bolster your ego, I'm asking you to do it to assist you in becoming mentally stronger than you are now.

Your initial success in this process isn't the end, but the beginning. Once you've lost the weight, the secret rests on maintaining healthful habits that keep the weight off. This is a lifestyle overhaul, and your level of mental toughness will determine whether you fail or succeed. I remember building the habit of lifting weights. I'd always trained for tennis, and I'd built the lean body I needed to be lightning-fast on the court. When I entered college, I wanted to gain ten-to-twenty pounds of muscle, so I started lifting weights six days a week. After six months of rigorous training, my body began to take shape. One of the best moments of recognition was the time I left the college gym after working out and was heading to my car. I had shorts on and my shirt off, and I walked into a clique of football players talking to some of the cheerleaders. The head cheerleader was in a few of my classes and she was gorgeous. Unfortunately, she never gave me a second look in class. As I walked through the group of them standing in the parking lot talking, though, she looked at me and said, "Aren't you in my sociology class?" and I said, "Yeah, I think so." And she said loudly in front of everyone, "God, you have a great body." I can't tell you the exhilaration I felt. Her remark was spoken more than thirty years ago and I can still feel the rush of adrenaline as I write this chapter. That's the power of recognition.

After that incident I worked out more ardently and three decades later I'm still doing it. I'm not saying the cheerleader's remark was the only reason for working out, but it was the first time anyone had ever recognized me for being muscular, and it felt great. The fact that she was the sexiest girl on campus didn't hurt, either. My point is I worked diligently to build my body so it looked good, and you're going to work just as hard to become a fat loser. Why not embrace the recognition, thank the person who recognized you, and let it serve as fuel for an already-blazing fire? By the time the compliments start, you'll deserve every one you receive.

"Fat losers embrace the recognition they receive because they deserve it, and they use it to motivate themselves to greater success."

Critical Thinking Question

ARE YOU MENTALLY AND EMOTIONALLY PREPARED FOR THE WAVE OF RECOGNITION YOU'LL RECEIVE WHEN YOU HIT YOUR WEIGHT-LOSS GOAL?

Action Step

Begin to mentally rehearse your responses to people showering you with compliments in order to be prepared and comfortable when it happens.

MENTAL-TOUGHNESS STRATEGY #77

PROGRAM YOURSELF FOR SUCCESS

Constructing new ways of thinking and converting them into habits is no easy task. As a matter of fact, it's one of the most difficult things to do, especially as you grow older and your habits are more firmly rooted. Most of us are programmed for mediocrity. Most people are smart, educated, and talented enough to be and do anything they desire. The potential is there, but it's rarely fulfilled, which leaves many people frustrated. The truth is most of us are capable of great success, yet few achieve it. The reason is largely one of negative programming by individuals and people in power. I remember meeting with my high school guidance counselor regarding my poor grades. She told me that attending college would be a waste of time. I'd never considered *not* going to college, and as an all-state tennis player my junior year of high school, I knew I'd be offered dozens of scholarships. I was perplexed by her negative remark, but most of all her attitude. After all, she was making a recommendation based on *grades* alone. She didn't know my talent or potential. Two years later, I was enrolled in college, earning straight A's on a scholarship.

The pastor leading our confirmation classes had never approved of me because he said I asked too many questions about the Bible and should just take it on faith. He told our class one day that we were born sinners and powerless without God, and I laughed out loud. I was ejected from the class and sent to the head pastor's office for punishment. I told the head pastor I thought the Bible was attempting to manipulate people and control them through fear-based brainwashing, and I was almost kicked out of the church and denied my confirmation after three years of classes.

One of my business professors in college told me how foolish it would be for anyone to start a business without major capital funding, and that we'd be better off working for someone else. And the list of unsound advice, brainwashing, and poor programming goes on.

You probably have as many examples of this kind of programming in your life as I do. Is it any wonder so many of us fail to obtain results? Most of us have been taking advice from well-intentioned people doling out egregious information. For the people aware of this societal phenomenon, those days are over. We know our programming is our responsibility, and it needs to be a reflection of the success we want to achieve. Bombarding your mind with positive messages of hope, inspiration, and motivation is a starting point. Another strategy is listening only to people with uplifting ideas that move us closer to our goals. Reprogramming yourself for success, though, requires time and opposes societal norms, but it works and is worth the effort for every area of your life where performance is important.

"Reprogramming yourself for success is critical to becoming a fat loser. When seventy percent of society is fat and becoming fatter, it's time to take action in the opposite direction."

Critical Thinking Question

HOW MANY OF YOUR HABITS, ACTIONS, AND BEHAVIORS ARE CONGRUENT WITH BECOMING HEALTHY AND FIT?

Action Step

Take inventory of the positive, life-affirming beliefs and habits you currently possess and make a commitment to upgrade them if necessary.

MENTAL-TOUGHNESS STRATEGY #78

CONTINUE TO LEARN

Every diet is different and each human body is too, which is the reason it's important to keep learning. Some diets are focused on calorie-counting; others work through a point- or carb-counting system. Whatever diet you choose, study it as much as possible to learn the nuances. This knowledge will make it easier to lose and maintain your weight. Exercise is another area about which to learn as much as you can. For example, I've discovered after years of working out that consistency is more important than the amount of time I spend in the gym. If you want to be a bodybuilder, this attribute doesn't apply. To become a fat loser and develop muscle in the process, consistency has been crucial to my success.

Everyone is a little different, so experiment with various regimens or seek help from a personal trainer. Reading health and fitness magazines can also be an excellent way to learn new techniques. The ultimate area in which to become educated about permanent weight loss is your mind. As you go through the weight-loss process, notice the aspects that motivate, de-motivate, and genuinely inspire you. Also become aware of your weaknesses and the traps into which you fall when you're tempted to cheat or quit. For example, my motivation to diet begins to decline if I miss a workout or two. It also de-motivates me to work out if I cheat on my diet. For me, dieting and exercise are psychologically interconnected, and it took a while for me to figure out the connection. Now I'm careful not to minimize the effect of one on the other. My greatest motivator occurs when my waist-to-chest ratio increases. In other words, my chest increases through regular workouts, and my waist size decreases. This ratio makes me look better and feel great. The more you know about the triggers that drive your behavior, the easier it is to control. Never stop learning and discovering new things about every aspect of this process. The more you know, the more fit you'll become.

"Fat losers never stop learning and growing. They know the secret to success is the intelligent application of specific knowledge."

Critical Thinking Question

ON A SCALE OF 1-7, 7 AS THE MOST, HOW MUCH DO YOU KNOW ABOUT YOUR DIET AND EXERCISE PROGRAM?

Action Step

Set a goal to learn one new fact every day about your diet and exercise program.

MENTAL-TOUGHNESS STRATEGY #79

BEWARE OF YOUR EMOTIONAL REACTIONS

To become mentally strong, control your emotions when pressured, stressed, or agitated. Emotional control is the essence of mental toughness, which is the reason it's critical to have it when you need it. Dieting is relatively easy once you make a decision to remain focused. No, you can't binge endlessly on your favorite foods or devour huge amounts of any food, but most diets offer solid food choices and eating them only requires light discipline. So you're going along swimmingly, losing weight and feeling great, and suddenly, out of the blue, an event occurs. You lose your job, your spouse wants a divorce, or a parent becomes gravely ill. Your life immediately goes into a tailspin, leaving you scrambling for a way to reduce the pain. Some people turn to liquor, others to drugs. But most of us use food to medicate and comfort ourselves. We do this unconsciously, but if you're on a diet, you begin to feel this overwhelmingly strong desire to eat non-nutritious foods. It's a form of self-medication, and it works temporarily while you're consuming the food. Afterwards, though, you feel worse than before because in addition to this terrible life event, you just added another problem.

I've never heard of anyone being happy that they cheated on their diet. The fun of cheating only lasts through the meal, and the more satiated you become the worse you feel. Major life events always pose a threat, but even minor forms of stress can be dangerous. I tore my anterior cruciate ligament (ACL) in the middle of a successful weight-loss journey, and the first thing I wanted to do after leaving the hospital was eat chips and salsa, which is not a recommended food on *anyone's* diet. I felt sorry for myself, and the chips would make me feel better. And they did, for the first *five minutes* I was eating them. Then I felt worse about my knee *and* my diet. Avoid these traps by becoming acutely aware of your emotional reactions to life events and the danger they pose. No one can avoid these kinds of events, but we can use our elevated awareness to derail our emotions and prevent them from destroying the momentum we worked so diligently to build.

"Fat losers know that fitness is always an uphill battle, and the most insidious enemy is emotion."

Critical Thinking Question

ON A SCALE OF 1-7, 7 AS THE BEST, HOW COMPETENT ARE YOU AT CONTROLLING YOUR EMOTIONS?

Action Step

List the ten most threatening scenarios or events that could threaten your diet.

MENTAL-TOUGHNESS STRATEGY #80

KNOW THE CLOCK IS TICKING

In our flagship program, Mental-Toughness University, we have a section called Sense Of Urgency that has caused major controversy. I used to call it the *Death Clock*, and it was a large cardboard display asking the question: "How many days do you have left?" I gotta be honest: it frightened people, but that wasn't the purpose. I created it to help people create a sense of urgency in their lives. The *Death Clock* reinforced the point that we don't live forever and the clock is always ticking. I used it for many years in speeches I delivered worldwide until I realized many people don't want to be reminded of their own mortality. This knowledge, however, doesn't change the fact that we are all mortal and only have so much time remaining. Endless dieting doesn't exist when there's an end. There is only a finite amount of time to become fit and healthy before the clock stops ticking and your heart stops beating.

This notion begs the question; if not now, when? In other words, if you're not going to be mentally strong enough to stay on the diet this time around, *when will you stay on it?* We only receive so many chances because we have only a certain amount of time remaining on the clock. The average man lives to seventy-five and the average woman to eight-one, but many people don't make it that long. Knowing this fact, the obvious critical-thinking question becomes, "What are you waiting for?" No one is coming to the rescue and time is growing shorter every day. You're not *preparing* for the game of life; you're *in* the game of life. Is there really any benefit to be gained by playing at half speed? And for those morbidly obese, your time may be limited due to the danger in which you've put yourself. Be warned that you're engaged in an emergency situation and your success may save your life. You need to take immediate action while you still have time. I don't know how much time you have, but right now you still have a chance. The purpose of becoming more aware of time is the sense of urgency it creates, motivating us to move forward fearlessly, and to seize the day. Become fit while you still have a choice. Remember that the clock is ticking.

"Fat losers know that life is temporary and now is the time to fulfill their desires."

Critical Thinking Question

HAVE YOU BEEN DIETING AS IF YOU HAVE ALL THE TIME IN THE WORLD?

Action Step

Calculate the number of days you have left if you live to be the average age.

MENTAL-TOUGHNESS STRATEGY #81

MAKE FITNESS SIMPLE

When I was training on the tennis tour, being fit was part of the job. After retiring, however, I had to learn new ways of staying fit, and frankly, it was a little overwhelming. I decided to keep it simple by engaging in the activities I enjoyed, such as weight-lifting, running, and walking. It's easier to follow exercise activities you enjoy. For example, my wife loves to play tennis. I taught her when we were dating, and she became a tennis fanatic. She belongs to tennis clubs in both states in which we reside and she plays five-to-six days a week. She's always had to watch her weight, and her enjoyment of tennis has helped her stay fit. The point of my story is that part of keeping fitness simple is finding a physical activity to enjoy.

The good news is that so many choices are available, from yoga to plyometrics to spinning classes. There's something for everyone. Like dieting, the secret is making it a habit that becomes part of your daily routine, like brushing your teeth. For example, if I don't work out for a couple of days, I start feeling sluggish and out of control, which is the result of interfering with a habitual behavior. I don't need to invest hours working out to fulfill the emotional and physical requirements; I only need forty-five to sixty minutes a day. I don't lift heavy weights and I don't do extreme exercises.

If you enjoy those types of exercises, then by all means engage in those activities. Unless you're training for the Olympics, moderate exercise is sufficient. So find a form of exercise you enjoy, keep it simple, remain consistent, and you'll become more fit every day.

"Fat losers stay fit through simple, consistent exercise. This habit keeps their minds fresh and their bodies strong."

Critical Thinking Question

HAVE YOU BUILT A LIFETIME HABIT OF ENJOYABLE, CONSISTENT EXERCISE?

Action Step

List five forms of exercise you might enjoy, and try each one in the next few weeks.

MENTAL-TOUGHNESS STRATEGY #82

EMBRACE SELF-RELIANCE

A disturbing narrative is circulating in America, and it could mark the beginning of the end. A growing segment of the population is rejecting the notion that individuals are responsible for their own behavior, results, and life in general. Some people call it the entitlement mentality, while others label it laziness. I call it the philosophy that could destroy America. At the heart of this cancerous ideology is a broken and bloated federal government promising people services it can't deliver and money it doesn't have. Both political parties are blameworthy. Both are addicted to spending money the country doesn't have with the idea that we can always print more. We're approaching eighteen trillion dollars in debt with absolutely no way to repay it, and the average American is oblivious to this oversight. So what does this problem have to do with becoming a fat loser? Simply put, it deals with *mindset*. This same mindset makes people fat. The idea you can become fat, suffer the sicknesses that follow, and rely on government, the medical establishment, or your family to pay for the consequences of your misbehavior, is irresponsible.

The solution focuses on turning this philosophy inside out by embracing self-reliance. This strategy demands you grow up emotionally, stop whining about being overweight and solve the problem. It also demands you accept full responsibility for becoming overweight, forgive yourself, and promise to become fit. Embracing self-reliance means understanding you're not only the problem, but also the *solution*. It requires you to take ownership of your life and stop waiting for a hero on a white horse to save you. The only person riding to the rescue is *you*, but only if you have the courage to stare objective reality straight in the face. The upside of this strategy is the freedom you feel as a self-reliant citizen who doesn't need the government, food companies, or outside entities in order to thrive. It may be too late to turn the country around, but you still have a chance to weave this thread into the fabric of your life. All it requires is a subtle shift in thinking.

"Fat people wait to be rescued. Fat losers know they are the only hero coming to save the day."

Critical Thinking Question

WHOSE FAULT IS IT THAT YOU'RE OVERWEIGHT?

Action Step

Post a sign on your refrigerator that reads: "Grow Up and Get Tough!" This note will remind you who's ultimately responsible for your eating habits.

MENTAL-TOUGHNESS STRATEGY #83

EMBRACE SEXUAL ENERGY

Americans are brainwashed from birth with puritanical programming about the meaning and practice of sex. Between non-comprehensive sex education in schools and the guilt-ridden religious doctrine of the church, is it any wonder Americans are so confused about sex? The physical, mental, and emotional energy of sex is the most powerful force on earth, yet it's been vilified in our so-called socially progressive culture. This outlook is not only foolish, but also removes the enjoyment from one of life's most precious gifts. Instead of denying the power of sexual energy, embrace it and reap the benefits of this beautiful aspect of life. Let's be honest, being fat doesn't inspire sexual energy in you or your partner. If big was truly beautiful, the modeling industry would have a bullpen of heavyweights wearing plus-sized clothing. The swimsuit edition of *Sports Illustrated* would also have three-hundred-pound females in tent-like swimsuits lying on the beach. Porn movies would filled with fat people having sex.

The truth reveals that fat is not beautiful, sexy, or healthful in any way, shape, or form. Being fat is ugly, unhealthful, and repulsive. I'm not saying these words to be *mean* to overweight people. I used to be one of them. I'm saying these words because it's true and no other public figure seems to be willing to say them. This isn't about hurting anyone's feelings; it's about waking up to the facts of life and solving the problems. Sexual energy is not only great for sex but can also be transmuted into ambition, attention, and even physical energy enabling you to reach the next level of success. Those who have ever had to take a cold shower to weaken the sexual energy pulsing through their bodies know the raw power with which we're dealing. Is there any other type of energy that requires a cold shower to squelch its fervor? If there is, I'm not aware of it. Becoming fit increases the volume on sexual energy unlike anything I've ever known. It has no equal. To call being fit an aphrodisiac is an understatement of considerable magnitude. Fit people *feel sexy, look sexy,* and *are sexy*. So if you think being fat is *not* costing you sex, or better sex, stop fooling yourself. Instead of trying to control and harness your sexual energy, embrace it fully and watch this fabulous flower of energy bloom. The more fat cells you lose, the sexier and more desirable you'll become.

"Fit people have better sex because they look and feel sexier than fat people. You can curse them or join them."

Critical Thinking Question

HAVE YOU DELUDED YOURSELF INTO BELIEVING THAT BEING OVERWEIGHT ISN'T NEGATIVELY IMPACTING YOUR SEX LIFE?

Action Step

Decide today to release yourself from the guilt and negative emotions you associate with sex and watch the positive energy flow like a running faucet. Give yourself permission to put the puritanical brainwashing behind you.

MENTAL-TOUGHNESS STRATEGY #84

GET EXCITED

When I was fat, I had no idea about the way my life would change once I became fit again. I had no frame of reference, no prior experience in this area of transition because I had always been extremely fit. You could say I never fully appreciated how marvelous it felt to be fit because I'd never been fat. My weight gain was so gradual I never noticed I was being robbed of my energy, enthusiasm, and vitality, until it returned. I was astonished at the remarkable way I felt and the immediate impact my weight loss had on every aspect of my life. I started playing tennis again, working out more intensely, and running more often. And the psychological benefits exceeded the physical ones. I found myself being more creative and able to sustain stronger concentration much longer. I made more money than ever before and I felt proud that I'd solved this irritating problem once and for all.

I experienced a feeling of calm and well-being I'd never previously felt. And eleven years later, I'm still reaping the benefits of that twelve-week drive. Now that's what I call a worthwhile investment. I want you to become excited about the life that awaits you as a fit person and the excitement about the way it's going to feel when you look in the mirror and marvel at your muscled, svelte, sexy body. Become excited about the elevated sense of self-confidence you'll experience as a fit person in a world of full of fat people. Become excited about the deep, positive psychological impact your success will have on you. You're weeks or months away from a life of fitness, success, and high self-esteem. Isn't it going to be wonderful? Becoming a fat loser isn't only about becoming fit; it's about *winning* in the game of life. And who doesn't want to enjoy victory?

"Fat people feel sluggish and slow. Fit people feel enthusiastic and energized."

Critical Thinking Question

HAVE YOU REALLY CONSIDERED THE IMPACT OF FITNESS ON YOUR OVERALL HAPPINESS?

Action Step

Invest one minute in the morning when you awaken and one minute at night before you fall asleep to think about the wondrous benefits that await you as a fit person.

MENTAL-TOUGHNESS STRATEGY #85

NEVER SAY DIE

One of the proudest moments I enjoyed as an athlete came from a story I heard after playing a hard-fought match. In 1982, I was playing in the finals of the Gatorade Open being held in Atlanta during the dog days of summer. I'd lived and trained in Chicago and was unaccustomed to the South's humidity. The match was really close, felt as though it had gone on forever, and I started to feel nauseous. It was five-to-five in the third set, and I suddenly started seeing double and becoming dizzy. My opponent began yelling at me, thinking I was stalling when I fell to the ground and vomited violently. I threw up seven times in five minutes, and the umpire told me he was stopping the match. I begged him to give me a minute and I'd continue, and my opponent agreed. A friend of mine was sitting next to my long-time coach, the tennis equivalent of Vince Lombardi. The coach didn't have blood flowing in his veins, he had *anti-freeze*. He was one of the toughest people I've ever known and a relentless disciplinarian. As I was stumbling around the court trying to regain my balance, I couldn't stop vomiting.

A doctor in the stands yelled, "Call the match. I'm a physician, and this kid has heat stroke. He needs to quit and get out of the sun. My friend told me later that the coach heard this comment and calmly said, "He'll never quit." And the physician overheard the coach and said, "Why not? This kid is sick and needs medical attention. Why won't he quit?" And the coach said with absolutely no emotion in his voice, "He doesn't know how." The physician was outraged and said, "How do you know?" And the coach said, "That's how I trained him. That's why he's a champion." I recovered my balance long enough to win seven-to-five in the last set and won the tournament. The coach never told me the story. My friend had overheard the conversation and shared it with me. Playing in one-hundred-degree weather with heatstroke isn't clever. After the match, I spent the night in the hospital being treated for dehydration and heatstroke. Today, that kind of coaching would be considered extreme and dangerous, but here's the point: I was trained to *never say die*. Quitting was surrendering, and surrendering was a *capital offense* to the coach. I know it sounds extreme, but it has served me well, and it will do the same for you. When the stakes are as high as living fit or dying fat, you need the never-say-die philosophy to ensure your success. The next time you tip the scale at a higher number than expected, can't seem to break through a stubborn and frustrating plateau, or have become tired of watching everyone around you eating your favorite food, here's my advice: never say die. They say that every dog has his day, and if you're tough enough, yours will come.

> *"Fat people give up when they get hungry. Fat losers never say die."*

Critical Thinking Question

ON A SCALE OF 1-7, 7 AS THE MOST EXTREME, HOW COMMITTED ARE YOU ON YOUR DIET TO THE NEVER-SAY-DIE PHILOSOPHY?

Action Step

Listen to Black Sabbath's 1978 classic hit "Never Say Die." This song is the theme on which this coaching philosophy is based.

MENTAL-TOUGHNESS STRATEGY #86

FOLLOW ROLE MODELS

One step on my journey to becoming a fat loser was identifying a role model to emulate. A few years earlier, I'd met a professional speaker and former competitor on the hit TV show, *American Gladiator*. His name was Michael Altshuler, and he was fit, *really* fit. Michael told me that to qualify as a gladiator he had to do thirty pull-ups in thirty seconds. I'm not sure if you've ever done pull-ups before, but not only are they extremely taxing, but doing thirty in thirty seconds is inhuman. I'd been doing pull-ups and chin-ups since high school, and I was well versed in both. But I knew doing that many in that time frame was something only a world-class fitness professional could accomplish. Michael was five years my senior, built like a brick, and had a thirty-one-inch waist. So he became the role model I followed, at least in spirit. I never asked him to coach or guide me, I merely thought about the choices he'd make before eating and exercising, and it inspired me to succeed.

I'd recommend you follow at least one role model, whether a personal trainer, friend, or a celebrity like Michael. Pick someone you admire for some specific attribute that motivates and inspires you. For example, another thing that inspired me about Michael, besides the pull-ups, was the size of his waistline. I was normally a thirty-two or thirty-three, but after becoming bloated I'd ballooned to a size thirty-six. None of my pants fit me properly, and I had my suits altered for speeches. I can't tell you how much this alteration aggravated me, and reducing my waist size became the most important aspect of my weight loss. I really didn't care how much I weighed as long as my waist size returned to a thirty-two or thirty-three. Working out had given me a healthful-sized chest, and combined with a small waist, I felt as svelte as a Swede in his prime.

Consider a specific body part your role model has mastered, but remain realistic in your goal. For instance, I knew I could reduce my waist, and I also knew I'd never be able to do thirty pull-ups in thirty seconds without years of effort. I only used the pull-up example to inspire me to work out, and it was successful. If you're an endomorph, don't post body pictures of Elle McPherson on your vision board. Genetics play a role in this process, so choose someone with your same body-type. Once you've selected your role models, make them a part of your *fitness consciousness*. When you feel like skipping a workout or cheating on your diet, ask yourself the actions your role models would take. This role-model selection is merely another psychological strategy on your road to fitness.

> *"Fat people follow other fat people. Fat losers follow role models that embody fitness success."*

Critical Thinking Question

DO YOU UNDERSTAND THE MOTIVATIONAL AND INSPIRATIONAL VALUE OF FOLLOWING ROLE MODELS?

Action Step

Give yourself a week to identify some examples and then select at least one fitness role model.

MENTAL-TOUGHNESS STRATEGY #87

STOP SAYING DIETS DON'T WORK

The biggest lie in the world about weight loss says "diets don't work." Even the medical community has perpetrated this lie, and the effect is a world of fat people growing fatter. Big money is made from disempowering people. The fact is that a healthful diet is simply an eating regimen you follow that serves your best interests. Diets work perfectly, every time. People don't always work the diet, but that doesn't mean the *diet* doesn't work. Diets are like budgets. If you stay on them, they are extremely effective. The missing ingredient of successful dieting is mental toughness, because that's all it takes to stay on a diet. Madison Avenue doesn't want you to be mentally tough because that eliminates the demand for the alternative profit-driven solution. The last thing the profiteers want is people becoming self-sufficient. They prefer that you are vulnerable, incapable of controlling your base desires, and therefore, susceptible to their offerings.

The church has done the same for 2,000 years. The message that you're hopeless without God is the most successful marketing campaign in history.

The government is another example. It creates entitlement programs for the masses under the guise that we're not intelligent enough to take care of ourselves without Big Brother's assistance. So it programs us to believe we'd perish without it and as a result, it becomes bigger and more powerful with every new administration, both democratic and republican. Oh, yes, and it taxes us to pay for it. Lawmakers want their constituents to be vulnerable in order to increase their influence, power, and control. And it works because most people don't pay close-enough attention to know they're being manipulated.

Admitting that diets work strips away all power from the medical community, pharmaceutical industry, and the entire weight-loss industrial complex. It's financial castration to a multi-billion-dollar industry, and that's the reason the lie is perpetuated. The masses continue believing it because it lets them off the hook for their own failure. Selling delusion and denial is an extremely profitable business. And because it feels good and absolves people of the burden of self-responsibility, business will always flourish. Your job as a mentally tough critical thinker means avoiding and rejecting the mind-traps of the masses. Diets *do* work. Do you?

"If you want to find the source of societal manipulation, follow the money trail. The purveyors are seeking power, money or both."

Critical Thinking Question

ON A SCALE OF 1-7, 7 AS THE MOST HOW COMFORTABLE ARE YOU WITH SAYING NO TO REQUESTS THAT DON'T SERVE YOUR BEST INTERESTS?

Action Step

Read my book *Die Fat or Get Tough: 101 Differences in Thinking between Fat People and Fit People*. This book will open your eyes to the false and destructive beliefs of fat people.

MENTAL-TOUGHNESS STRATEGY #88

RADIATE SUCCESS

There's an old saying, "Nothing succeeds like success." Like most adages, it's stood the test of time because it's *true*. I've been interviewing successful people around the world for more than thirty years, and it's always fascinated me the way they seem to glide effortlessly from one success to the other. This isn't *completely* accurate, though. We all know that successful people *fail* most of the time. The difference is every time they are knocked down they stand back up and start over with more information, knowledge, and experience that eventually leads them to success. After spending three decades with these people, I've concluded it's their level of thinking that empowers them to behave this way and it's the secret to their success. By thinking a certain way, successful people radiate success. They are not only successful, they *are* success. They embody success. They bring successful thinking to their every action, whether it's making a million, cleaning the kitchen, or staying on a diet. Their mindset guarantees they will be successful in any undertaking. They may experience failure in the short term, but through persistent effort and a positive attitude they eventually fulfill their desires. This is the reason the rich become richer, the fit, fitter, and the happy, happier. It's also the reason why the poor become poorer, the fat, fatter, and the sad, sadder. One group of people is no smarter than another, but their mindset and attitudes are a world apart.

Radiating success means thinking positively, searching for validation in everyone and every situation, and doing things the way successful people do them. One of my mentors is a professional speaker named Jim Cathcart, and Jim asks his audiences to consider the following question, "How would the person you want to *be* do the thing you're about to do?" It's one of the most important questions you can ask yourself in becoming a fat loser. Ask yourself that question at every meal and exercise session to help you build the habit of successful thinking. Remember that success isn't a "sometimes" situation; it's an *all-the-time* event. That doesn't mean you're going to be perfect and never make mistakes. To err is human. But the idea centers on bringing success to every facet of your life, including your quest for fitness. Every success you experience along the way positively impacts everything else you attempt to do.

"Fat people radiate failure. Fat losers radiate success. One group is no better than the other, but each one's different thinking creates opposite results."

Critical Thinking Question

ON A SCALE OF 1-7, 7 AS THE BEST, HOW OFTEN WOULD PEOPLE CLOSE TO YOU SAY THAT YOU RADIATE SUCCESS?

Action Step

Inventory your thinking by asking yourself whether or not you radiate success in any situation. This assessment will help you form the habit and reap the rewards.

MENTAL-TOUGHNESS STRATEGY #89

BECOME DESENSITIZED

One of my favorite places in the world is Sydney, Australia. I've been delivering speeches, conducting seminars, and appearing in the media *down under* for years. I've been interviewed on every major morning TV show in Sydney, and the press and public have always been congenial to me. One thing I've encountered in Oz, as the Aussies call it, is the *"Tall Poppy Syndrome."* This syndrome occurs when someone tries to outshine the others, in other words, attempts to become a taller poppy in the field, so to speak, and is brandished by his classmates or countrymen. The ambitious people wanting to better themselves are considered exhibitionists attempting to become taller poppies, and every effort is made to dissuade them and bring them back to the same height or success as the others. This syndrome is a defeatist one in the Australian culture, and the reason some Aussies connect more with American ideals. Overall, American culture embraces ambition and rewards people for success. However, sometimes friends and family can become resentful of the efforts and successes of someone close to them. It's pure jealousy, and the net result is they either ignore the striver or attempt to disempower him. When you're on the path to losing weight, becoming healthier, and building a better life, you would think that the people who care about you would support you. But sometimes they don't, and oftentimes this negativity destroys people's goals and dreams.

You tell people you're going on a diet and they say, "Oh, you don't need to lose weight. You look fine" or you join a health club and they say, "you're going to look like a bulging bodybuilder." Of course, these responses have nothing to do with you or your goal; they are merely the reflection of envious mindsets comparing your efforts and results with theirs. The solution is what psychologists call "Systematic Desensitization." It sounds complex, but it's actually quite simple: it means that over time, you'll become desensitized to the words to which you're repeatedly exposed. So the more often people tell you that "Diets don't work," "Health clubs are for bodybuilders" and "You're just going to gain all of it back" the less it affects you. One day you wake up and no longer feel the impact of their words. It's one of the most liberating experiences, and like all strategies, it transfers to every aspect of your life. You begin listening to people who empower you, while learning to ignore everyone else. The bottom line is it's your diet, your body, and your life. Other people's opinions may be well-intentioned, but they're not important if they fail to empower you.

"Desensitizing yourself to the reactions and opinions of others is the great secret of successful people."

Critical Thinking Question

HOW HAVE THE NEGATIVE OPINIONS AND REACTIONS OF OTHER PEOPLE IMPACTED YOU IN THE PAST DURING THE DIETING PROCESS?

Action Step

Every time you hear negative words about dieting examine how much they are affecting you.

MENTAL-TOUGHNESS STRATEGY #90

KNOW YOUR BELIEF IS NOT REQUIRED

In the world of personal development and self-help psychology, *beliefs* reign supreme. The idea is that beliefs drive behavior, so if you want to change your behavior, start with your beliefs. After thirty years of studying, writing, and speaking on this subject, I can state with authority that the concept is completely accurate, with one major exception: linear processes that *only* require action. One example cites becoming more organized. All that's required is the willingness to follow a few simple steps to succeed. Another is learning to dress for success. A few basic tips and you're on your way. Maybe the most important linear process in self-improvement is weight loss. If you follow a nutritious diet and are faithful to your exercise program, you *will* become fit, and you're belief system has *nothing* to do with it. More simply stated, your belief is not *required*. That's the beauty of the logical, linear part of life. In a world filled with uncertainty, two plus two always equals four, the law of gravity will always be true, and rain will always turn to snow when the temperature drops below thirty-two degrees Fahrenheit. These are all examples from the linear world, and their beauty lies in their simplicity and predictability. The nonlinear world, however, is much larger and more complex and usually requires major belief-changes to move to the next level.

For example, becoming rich through linear thinking is possible, but without the belief that you have what it takes, it's improbable that you'll take action to manifest it. It's easy to tell someone the strategy to becoming a better spouse, but without a change in belief or an explanation, the behavior will likely remain the same. Loving and respecting your fellow humans makes logical sense, but until you believe your fellow humans are worthy of love, the behavior is jeopardized. These two are the different worlds of linear and nonlinear circumstances. I've detailed them in this way to emphasize and clarify the simplicity and straightforward nature of weight loss. The mystery of the process reveals that *there is no mystery*. Do the work and you'll obtain results. If you're a woman, it may take longer than if you're a man. If you're an endomorph, it will probably take you longer than it would a mesomorph. If you're older, it will probably take longer than someone younger. If you have emotional issues, travel a great deal, or have a houseful of kids to nurture, it will probably be more difficult. No matter the struggle you have to endure, however, you'll *eventually* succeed. In the linear world, your belief is not required, only your consistent action.

"Fat people believe dieting is complicated. Fat losers know it's a simple, linear process."

Critical Thinking Question

DO YOU THINK YOU HAVE TO CHANGE YOUR BELIEFS IN ORDER TO BECOME FIT?

Action Step

Begin to separate the linear and nonlinear areas of self-improvement to clarify the actions required to succeed in both.

MENTAL-TOUGHNESS STRATEGY #91

TAKE PRIDE IN YOUR BODY

Was there ever a time in your life when you were proud of your body? I never considered this concept until I got fat. Suddenly, I was shy about removing my shirt, wearing a bathing suit, or sleeping naked. It was a completely new experience for me, and I didn't like it one bit. I'd always been proud of my body, but I was so used to being fit I took it for granted. One saying states it perfectly: "You don't know what you have till it's gone"? I felt that way until I became a fat loser and regained my svelte shape. I didn't realize what I'd been missing. People treat you differently when you're fat.

We're all taught as youngsters not to judge a book by its cover, yet we all do. Contrary to popular political correctness, fat people are seen as lazy, sloppy, and unorganized. *It doesn't mean they are*; it simply means they are *perceived* that way. They are instantly marginalized and judged for their failure to control their eating habits. They're passed over for jobs and passed up for promotions, all because of the stigmas, false or otherwise, that are part and parcel of being fat. I'm not saying it's right, but this is reality, and no amount of wishful thinking will change it. I confess to being guilty of this perception in the past. In the course of my career, I've hired hundreds of people, but very few of them were overweight. My mother wouldn't be proud of the reason I passed over the fat candidates, but the truth is I questioned their level of self-discipline. Before you start throwing rocks, ask yourself if you've ever done the same or at least considered it. I'm not proud of it, but I'm also not saying the thought won't cross my mind the next time I hire someone. How could it not?

No one looks at fat people and thinks, *"Wow, I'll bet those people are really in control of their lives."* Perhaps this person suffers from an eating disorder or is in therapy for gaining weight because of sexual abuse as a child. Unfortunately, a small percentage of people *are* struggling with those kinds of issues. But if you don't know that, you instantly assume a person is fat for no obvious reason save laziness. On the other side of the spectrum, you see really fit people cross your path and your first thought is, *"Wow, those people really take care of themselves. They must have high self-esteem and strong self-discipline."* It may be true or not, but oftentimes the first impression is all you have. I remember hiring a sales person years ago after interviewing over thirty people. It was late Friday afternoon and I was tired. He was my last interview of the week and I told my secretary to send him into my office. This guy, about fifty years old, walked through the doorway, and looked like a Greek god. He had a big chest, small waist, and a serious handshake. And the first thought crossing my mind was *this guy is proud of his appearance and that's the kind of salesperson I want representing me.* He said he'd been on a heart-healthy diet for years and adhered religiously to four-to-five light workouts a week. Then he placed a lynchpin in the interview by saying, "Mr. Siebold, I'm proud of the accomplishments in my life. I have a beautiful family, a growing net worth, and a healthful lifestyle. I love your work and I can sell it. If you'll give me the chance, I'll bring the same level of pride to this job that I bring to every facet of my life." I hired him on the spot, and he broke every sales record. My point is to consider the role pride plays in your fat-loser journey. If you take pride in your body, other people will notice it and see you in a different light. More important, you'll see *yourself* in a different light.

"Fat people are ashamed of their bodies. Fat losers are proud. The world sees the difference and makes judgments accordingly."

Critical Thinking Question

ON A SCALE OF 1-7, 7 AS THE MOST PROUD, HOW PROUD ARE YOU OF YOUR BODY?

Action Step

Think about the work your body needs to feel pride in your appearance.

MENTAL-TOUGHNESS STRATEGY #92

CELEBRATE WEIGHT LOSS

The three stages of weight loss are as predictable as they are important. If you know what they are and when to expect them, your fat-loser journey will be much more enjoyable. Instead of simply moving through the stages, I suggest you celebrate each one as you experience it. They all have value, and you'll have fond memories of them if you see their lessons as stages to celebrate as opposed to simply enduring them. The first one is the *excitement* stage. This is the time when you start your new diet and exercise program, and you're excited about the look and feel of your new body in the future. You're looking forward to the vast number of benefits awaiting you at the finish line, and you're feeling proud of yourself for undertaking the journey. This stage is a blast of emotion and it's a great deal of fun. Celebrate it. It's exciting, but it's short.

The next stage is the *season of pain*, beginning just as the excitement stage ends. The catalysts are usually cravings, hunger pangs, and loss of your favorite foods. The catalyst is largely irrelevant, because sooner or later, you'll move into this stage regardless of your strength or commitment. Becoming a fat loser requires major habit change, and old habits don't appreciate being replaced. Eventually you'll experience their wrath. The *season of pain* is the stage of uncomfortable uncertainty, and it's filled with physical, mental, and emotional discontent. This stage begins when you question whether or not you made the right decision, while seriously considering turning back. The uncertainty comes from never having succeeded at this task before or having succeeded only to relapse. You may begin with quick weight loss and suddenly hit a plateau. Or maybe the losses are slow from the beginning and you can't figure out the reason why. You may lose several pounds and suddenly regain them. The possible scenarios are endless. The *season of pain* is frustrating, irritating, and annoying, but if you're tough enough to take it, you'll move to the final stage.

The *knowing* stage is the phase in which you know you're going to succeed. It's the point in a race when you can see the finish line. It's the phase of a romantic relationship when you realize you're in love. It's the stage in business when it becomes evident you're going to become rich. All the questions are answered and the doubt disappears. Even though the journey is still in progress and you may have months to complete it, you know with absolute certainty that it *will* happen. This feeling creates a psychological tidal wave that can't be stopped, and it's a tremendous feeling to experience that level of certainty around a goal you were uncertain you could accomplish.

All three stages are necessary, and each one should be celebrated. After all, the victory without the struggle is not much of a victory, is it?

Celebrating the excitement of the *knowing* stage is easy, but celebrating the *season of pain* is the secret. If you learn to see suffering and pain in the same way you see excitement and certainty, you'll conclude that one can't exist without the other. All three stages are integral pieces of the puzzle, and all three should be celebrated.

"Celebrate all three stages of becoming a fat loser and you will appreciate your success even more."

Critical Thinking Question

HAVE YOU EVER CONSIDERED THE PSYCHOLOGICAL IMPACT OF CELEBRATING PAIN?

Action Step

Create a list of the different psychological struggles you may experience on your fat-loser journey. Acknowledgement alone reduces the level of suffering you'll experience.

MENTAL-TOUGHNESS STRATEGY #93

DON'T BELIEVE PROPAGANDA

In the spring of 2013, the American Medical Association held a press conference in Chicago following their annual meeting, and formally declared obesity a disease. CNN called me within minutes and invited me on the air to comment on this so-called claim. Since 2009, when *Die Fat or Get Tough* was published, I'd completed hundreds of interviews preaching to millions of people, advocating self-responsibility. The press knew I'd refute the AMA's claim, an organization few people are willing to confront publicly. In the next few days, my publicist was inundated with phone calls and emails requesting interviews on this development.

I completed as many interviews as possible, but the AMA casts a huge shadow and wields much more power than an author shouting with a single voice. In essence, the AMA gave fat people permission to be overweight because obesity is a disease they can't control. That statement is untrue, but the masses are emotionally vulnerable and likely to believe the messages of influential organizations and authoritative people. The AMA ought to be ashamed for exacerbating a problem they should be on the leading edge of solving. The truth is, however, their profit motive for making this claim doesn't affect someone like you proactively taking matters into your own hands and systematically solving the problem. The masses will suffer the consequences of the AMA's actions, but you won't unless you buy into their profit-driven propaganda. You see, declaring obesity a disease isn't about the truth; it's about *money*.

If obesity is a disease, doctors can bill insurance companies for diagnosing it and prescribing a cure. The comment that the AMA has made is so obvious it's embarrassing, and another reason to distrust any organization with a profit motive attached to its advice. As I mentioned earlier, Marcus Welby is dead. In other words, the days of blindly trusting your doctor are over. Doctors should be viewed with the same skepticism as any other profiteer. It's sad, but true. If you want to uncover the motive for similar self-serving propaganda, follow the money trail. It's not complicated, but buying into it could be costly. Instead, remain mentally steadfast and *think for yourself*. Doctors are experts with specialized knowledge, but they aren't above taking the low road of deceptive sales and marketing tactics. People of influence use propaganda tactics because they convince the masses. Critical thinkers will always see through it, ignore the false message, and chart their own courses.

"Fat losers are critical thinkers who consider all of the criteria and reach their own conclusions."

Critical Thinking Question

ARE YOU THINKING FOR YOURSELF OR ALLOWING OTHERS TO THINK FOR YOU?

Action Step

Until you're satisfied with the evidence to substantiate them, decide to bring skepticism to all claims about dieting and fitness.

MENTAL-TOUGHNESS STRATEGY #94

THINK CRITICALLY

In the self-improvement world, positive thinking has always reigned supreme. As with any movement containing real value, though, it continues to evolve and become more sophisticated. There's no better example than the evolution from positive to critical thinking. Positive thinking is an emotionally-charged process seeking the good in everyone and everything. The upside is that it leads to enhanced relationships, a heightened sense of well-being, and a happier overall existence. The downside, however, is that the emotional foundation clouds judgment and compromises a person's decision-making ability.

It also views negative thinking as the enemy, when negative thinking is as valuable in certain situations as positive thinking. For example, positive thinking works well when you have to travel to New York City on business in the dead of winter and would rather be in Palm Beach. The positive thinker simply looks for the good in the situation and the result is an improved attitude and overall disposition. Negative thinking works well when you land at La Guardia and are approached by a suspicious stranger wanting you to follow him to the parking garage. Positive thinking in this scenario may get you killed, and only skeptical, negative thinking may prevent it. The king of the hill is critical thinking, which is emotionless thinking that arrives at conclusions and decisions based on greater criteria, evidence, and logic. The reason it's an important part of your journey to becoming a fat loser is that losing weight is a process loaded with emotion. Human beings are emotional creatures sensitive about their bodies. Many of us see becoming fat as a personal failure and berate ourselves for it. The weight-loss industry capitalizes on this view in many ways, the most prominent of which is selling the idea that you can't lose weight without them. The truth is the only person you need to solve this problem is you. Does that mean you shouldn't hire a coach, join a weight-loss support group, or go on a pre-packaged food diet? No. All of these activities have value. I'm simply suggesting you engage in critical thinking and see the process for what it is. When I worked at Nutrisystem we helped a great many people. I also had great success with the Atkins Diet and Weight Watchers. Many nutritious diets are available, but critical thinking says all you need to become fit is intelligent decision-making around food choices and the mental toughness to make them. Millions of fat losers have never enrolled in a formal diet plan. They simply use critical thinking to chart their courses to healthful eating and suitable exercise habits. Others join a more formally structured diet. Use the one that works for you, and remember the real secret to your success is *you*.

"Fat losers rarely allow their emotions to cloud their eating and exercising decisions."

Critical Thinking Question

ARE YOU MAKING FOOD CHOICES BASED ON YOUR THOUGHTS OR FEELINGS?

Action Step

For the next twenty-four hours, document the thinking that led you to decide the foods to eat, and determine if critical or emotional thinking is dominating your decision-making process.

MENTAL-TOUGHNESS STRATEGY #95

STOP APPROVAL ADDICTION

Addiction is debilitating. It entices and then strangles you. It makes you feel as if you have no control. The most popular addictions are drugs and alcohol, but according to some experts, the most common is the *approval of others*. That's right, many if not most of us are addicted to the approval of other people. We care so much about people's impressions of us that it crosses over to addiction. Behind this addiction is the time when we were children needing something from adults and their approval of our behavior was the key to getting it. It worked for us in childhood, and most of us unconsciously continue seeking approval as adults.

How many people married the spouses their parents liked the most, or had children because their parents wanted grandkids, or majored in a certain subject because a relative strongly suggested it? I spent my summer breaks in college working in the machinery-moving industry because most of my extended family has been in that business for decades. Not only was I dreadful at it, but I also disliked it. I worked there because I wanted family approval. Many people waste their lives working for approval, and in some cultures, it's expected that you follow family tradition regardless of your personal happiness. It's an outdated, archaic formula for disaster, but the sad truth is it afflicts the masses.

Are you dieting to improve your health, or are you seeking others' approval? Do you want that bikini body to boost your self-esteem or because your lover wants it? During my two years of research interviewing fat and fit people, I met a small percentage of fat people who didn't mind being overweight. Of course their doctors wanted them to lose weight for health reasons, but other than that, they didn't mind looking at themselves in the mirror. I won't pretend to understand their satisfaction with being fat, but it was their lives. My point is if you're going to become a fat loser, don't do it because I say so, or society or anyone else says so. Do it for *you*.

Approval addiction is based on the idea that other people are seriously concerned with our actions, and studies reveal that most people are *far more worried about their own lives*. This is as it should be, but approval addicts act as though the world is taking great interest in them. I know because I used to be one, and after learning about approval addiction, I decided to live life my way, on my terms, and let other people think whatever they wanted. It's been the most liberating decision I've ever made. I love being fit because it provides a feeling of satisfaction. I enjoy the way my body feels in clothes at my ideal weight, and the positive feelings transfer to every area of my life. I don't eat well or exercise faithfully for anyone else. I do it for me. What about you? For whom are you losing weight? The more honestly and accurately you can answer that question, the more successful you'll be in the process and the happier you'll be with the end result.

"The masses live their lives for others, desperately seeking approval. The great ones live their lives on their own terms and place little importance on other people's opinions."

Critical Thinking Question

ON A SCALE OF 1-7, 7 AS THE MOST ADDICTED, HOW ADDICTED ARE YOU TO THE APPROVAL OF OTHERS?

Action Step

Inventory your reasons for wanting to be fit and determine if you're doing it for yourself or others.

MENTAL-TOUGHNESS STRATEGY #96

STOP WHINING

My late business partner, the great Bill Gove, delivered this funny line to audiences for more than fifty years, "do you know the difference between the average person and a litter of puppies? The difference is that after seven days the puppies stop whining." Most of us waste too much time complaining about hunger and not being able to eat favorite foods. I hate to admit it, but I've traveled the same road. During my first dieting attempt, I griped to my wife about the process, and the more I grumbled the more difficult it became. I was literally talking myself into believing it was more difficult to stay on the diet than it actually was. So I stopped moaning, and it became *easier*. I replaced complaining with talking about the excitement of being on the road to fitness and a more healthful life. I wish I could say I meant those words, but in the beginning, I was simply *mouthing* them, knowing my feelings would eventually follow my words. That's the way the brain works. For better or worse, it's a programmable machine. It seeks congruency, and if you lie to it long enough, it will believe almost anything until the belief is interrupted with critical, emotionless thinking. Look no further for the proof of this claim than the world's 4,500 religions and the spectacular mythology they perpetuate. The secret to the success of these cults is early indoctrination; so by the time these children are old enough to think independently, they've been robbed of the ability to do so. That's the way we convince Ivy-League-educated PhDs, brilliant business people, and influential world leaders to believe in talking snakes, virgin birth, and other wildly outrageous claims that have no evidence to support them. These people do not lack education or intelligence. They've been brainwashed from birth to believe the *unbelievable*. It's the reason people fly planes into buildings and blow themselves up with bombs. These smart people have been systematically programmed since childhood to believe things as adults that not even a precocious fourth-grader would believe.

Programming can be healthful, however, and replacing any whining that remains in your self-talk can reduce the stress and suffering you experience in the process. If your self-talk is strong enough, it can propel you to fitness even faster. Whining is a waste of time and nobody cares that you're craving unhealthful foods. Grow up, get mentally tough, and talk about your diet like an adult.

"Fat people whine about being fat while simultaneously continuing to eat like fat people. Fat losers stop whining, eat like intelligent adults, and become fit."

Critical Thinking Question

ARE YOU WHINING LIKE A CHILD OR WINNING LIKE AN ADULT?

Action Step

For the next twenty-four hours, when you catch yourself whining, immediately replace it with a more empowering message.

MENTAL-TOUGHNESS STRATEGY #97

BEGIN DIETING FOR LIFE

Dieting is like the used-car business: it has gained a bad reputation. Somehow, over the years, someone sold the masses on the idea that dieting was a short-term, unhealthful, and futile process to be avoided at all costs. It amazes me that a single person or small group can state their preferences and a few years later it's viewed as conventional wisdom. The advertising industry is a great example. It airs a commercial with bikini models, frolicking along the beach playing volleyball and drinking beer. I get it; guys love bikini models and guys love beer. It's a game of association. What do beer and bikini models have to do with each other in reality? If these women drank beer, they wouldn't be bikini models. We know this logically, but most people think emotionally.

Organized religion is the most extreme example. More than 4,500 documented religions exist worldwide, and they collectively worship many thousands of gods. I've spent years studying them and the stories are so unbelievable that the real miracle is the way people convince themselves to believe any of it. It's mythology masquerading as historical fact. This is the danger of emotionally-fueled thinking that ignores logic. Dieting is just another example whereby the world has been sold a complete fabrication, stating that diets don't work. The truth is diets work perfectly every time. Because people don't stay on diets doesn't mean they don't work. Blaming your diet for failing you is like blaming your budget when you exceed it. It's irrational, and the irrationality is created through emotion.

Emotion plays an important role in dieting, and that's using it for motivation. Your dream of looking like a million bucks at your next class reunion is a prime example. Emotion drives people to push past pain. It's a powerful psychological performance tool. The problem arises when it comes to decision-making; emotion makes smart people act stupidly. That's the reason they can be manipulated to believe the unbelievable, even if they've earned a doctorate degree from Harvard. Logic tells us that not only do diets work, but also they should be followed for a lifetime. Healthful eating and exercise habits aren't a hobby; they're a way of life. Again, it's no different than a budget, except you're substituting food for money. Even billionaires have budgets, because no matter how much money you have, you want to be a good steward and not waste it foolishly. The amount of money you have is irrelevant to the equation, just as your fitness is irrelevant to the dieting equation.

Do you really believe the world's sexiest supermodels aren't on strict diets? I walked the red carpet at the Academy Awards a few months ago with Catherine Zeta-Jones, and I'll bet you anything she's a professional dieter. No one stays *that* fit without the discipline of dieting. So I suggest something you already know: don't believe everything you hear and read on the Internet. Diets work and you need to maintain an organized, healthful diet for the rest of your life. If you ignore the masses and heed this advice, you'll live a more healthful, happier life, not to mention you'll look fabulous through every decade.

"Emotional thinking makes smart people stupid. Use logic to steer your diet and emotion to motivate you to maintain it."

Critical Thinking Question

DO YOU SEE YOUR DIET AS A SHORT-TERM SOLUTION OR A LONG-TERM LIFESTYLE?

Action Step

Take stock of your diet and be sure it's a healthful, long-term lifestyle as opposed to an unhealthful, quick way to shed a few pounds. If you're uncertain, consult your physician.

MENTAL-TOUGHNESS STRATEGY #98

START CELEBRATING

Once you decide to become a fat loser, the heart of the process is over before it begins. It's not over *technically*, but it is *emotionally*. The toughest part of becoming fit is deciding to do the work it takes to succeed. The rest is merely being mentally tough enough to adhere to your decision. The time to start celebrating is immediately after you've made the decision. Celebrating puts you in a pleasurable state of mind and creates a positive association. Celebrate the fact that you have the courage to accept becoming fat and the awareness to understand that you are the solution. Celebrate that idea that in a world of fat people, you're going to become fit and reap untold advantages. Celebrate the transfer effect that's going to happen when your fitness success positively impacts every area of your life without extra effort. Celebrate the honor you're going to feel as you become a role model for others struggling with their own weight issues.

You're going to become a beacon of hope for family, friends, and strangers who are inspired when they see you walking down the street. Celebrate the pride you're going to experience when you appear in public and hear people whispering about your slim good looks. Celebrate the impact you're fitness success will have on your children and their friends. And the list goes on. The benefits of being fit when most people are fat are substantial and worthy of celebration. Don't wait to celebrate, start immediately and let it empower you with psychological and emotional momentum.

Celebrate when you're feeling satisfied on the diet and celebrate when you're hungry and craving junk food. You're celebrating because you're in the game, fighting the fight in an area of life in which most people have given up.

Being tough enough to struggle through the pain and suffering of this process will provide a surge of self-esteem it's difficult to earn in any other way. There's no faster way to feel good about yourself than setting a big goal and achieving it, and the harder you have to fight to win, the greater the boost to your self-esteem. I'm not wishing you any greater struggle than you must endure to succeed, but the bigger the obstacle, the greater the victory. The easy fights in life are quickly forgotten. The difficult ones stay with you and become a source of pride. So celebrate now and work to make it happen. By deciding to succeed, you're already on your way.

"Fat people eat themselves into depression. Fat losers celebrate their success from the start and find happiness and excitement every day as they move closer to victory."

Critical Thinking Question

HAVE YOU STARTED CELEBRATING YOUR SUCCESS, OR ARE YOU STILL DECIDING ON THE PRICE YOU'RE WILLING TO PAY TO ACHIEVE IT?

Action Step

Create three new nonfood ways to celebrate your success.

MENTAL-TOUGHNESS STRATEGY #99

START MOTIVATING

Now that you're on your way to becoming a fat loser, become an *ambassador* of fitness. As your success becomes self-evident, you'll have the opportunity to motivate and inspire others. This ambassadorship will not only help others, but will also make you feel positive and keep you on track. I remember hearing my fitness role model, Michael Altshuler, talk about how good it feels to be fit and it motivated me to keep moving forward. I remember him discussing the way he prioritized his workouts and didn't let anything interfere, and it inspired me to do the same. After I wrote *Die Fat or Get Tough*, I participated in dozens of TV interviews worldwide attempting to motivate people with this mental-toughness approach. The directness of the message angered some people, shocked others, and the rest embraced it. I was able to deliver this message to more than fifty million people through the media, and it motivated me to stay on track.

Your success in this process is not only about you, but also about everyone coming in *contact* with you. And if you choose to embrace your role as a motivator, the impact you have on other people could change your life while improving theirs. For example, in 2001, I attended Hugh Hefner's seventy-fifth birthday party in Miami Beach, and I was astounded at the number of fit people. Every year Hef holds his annual Halloween party at the Playboy Mansion, hosting two thousand of the fittest bodies I've ever seen. I'm talking about women *and* men. Of all the parties I've attended at the Playboy Mansion, I can't remember seeing a fat person. The people attending these parties are rich, fit, and happy, and it's incredibly motivating to be in a room with that much success.

When it comes to fitness, they're no different from average people. No matter their wealth or fame, they still have to follow their diets and exercise programs to maintain fitness. Becoming a motivator for others will make your fat-loser journey easier and more enjoyable. Capitalize on this created momentum and you will arrive at your ideal weight much more quickly.

"Fat losers leverage the momentum that being a motivator creates to inspire themselves and others."

Critical Thinking Question

ON A SCALE OF 1-7, 7 AS THE BEST, HOW MUCH OF A MOTIVATOR ARE YOU TO OTHERS WHEN IT COMES TO WEIGHT LOSS AND FITNESS?

Action Step

Just for today, become a motivator for fitness success and see the way it impacts you. Then decide if the benefits are worth building it into a daily habit.

MENTAL-TOUGHNESS STRATEGY #100

EMBRACE YOUR SUCCESS

I grew up in the northwestern suburbs of Chicago, and the culture was one of pure Midwestern modesty. We weren't taught to embrace our successes. People who did were seen as conceited, overconfident, or egotistical. While some benefits apply to this modesty approach, the drawbacks are substantial. For example, during my twelve years on the junior tennis circuit, I won fifty-seven titles, ranked as high as #2 in singles and #1 in doubles. Years later, in my mid-thirties, I was discussing my junior tennis career with my dad, when he said, "you can't really see it as much of a success." Those were his exact words, which I'll never forget. He had always been supportive of my tennis career. He'd invested thousands of dollars in lessons, travel expenses, and other associated costs of being on the circuit. When it comes to success, however, the Midwestern mindset is tempered with modesty as the main goal, even to the point of reverse distortion. Success is a relative term, and mine was substantial compared to most junior players. I consider my junior career a success, but only in recent years have I arrived at this conclusion. I've learned to shake the chains of false modesty and embrace the success I've enjoyed in different facets of my life. This acceptance has had an enormous impact on my life, and I'm suggesting it for your consideration. As you become more successful as a fat loser and begin receiving accolades, embrace your success by thanking people for their recognition. Be proud that you've accomplished a feat most people do not and one the medical community has all but abandoned. Modesty in certain situations is appropriate and even refined, but it's empowering to embrace the success you've earned. After all, no one can lose weight for you. Through mental toughness and self-discipline, *you* made it happen, and you shouldn't be afraid to acknowledge this fact. A team of people can support you, but in the end, you're ultimately responsible for your results. So embrace your success and enjoy the feeling of being a winner in a game most people lose.

"Fat losers enjoy the spoils of their success and aren't afraid to acknowledge it."

Critical Thinking Question

HAVE YOU GIVEN YOURSELF THE CREDIT YOU DESERVE FOR EMBRACING FITNESS?

Action Step

In the next twenty-four hours, fully embrace the success you've had in the weight-loss process and experience the way it feels.

STEVE SIEBOLD

MENTAL-TOUGHNESS STRATEGY #101

GUARD THE DOOR

As I've said throughout this book, major habit-change is difficult work. Eliminating those unhealthful eating habits and establishing new ones is no small task. The good news is once you've fought the good fight and succeeded, you only need to stay alert in situations that threaten to put the old habits back in place. It's as though you've fought the war, replaced the bad habits with good ones, and now you must *stand guard at the door*. And figuratively speaking, you should be armed with a machine gun. Don't allow anyone or anything through that door to resurrect those bad habits. Some people call this maintenance, or keeping the weight off. I see it as taking over a territory and guarding it with your life. The longer you guard it, the easier it becomes as the new habits take root and begin to grow. After a while your guard duties will diminish, but you'll always be in danger. After ten years of guarding the door of my eating habits, I'm still tempted once in a while to gorge on a hot-fudge sundae or eat a whole bag of chips. I rarely give into the lure of bad habits, but the *temptation* is there. The good news is I don't physically or emotionally crave these foods anymore, so it's easier to guard against a weak feeling of desire than an overpowering one.

The most important aspect of guarding the door is the overall impact of letting your guard down from time to time. Recently I visited Beverly Hills, celebrating my wife's fiftieth birthday. We enjoyed a few drinks at a restaurant and later ordered German chocolate cake for dessert. We haven't ordered dessert at a restaurant in months, so we let our guard down and gorged on cake. Besides giving us stomachaches, I gained two pounds and she gained three. The next day I had dessert on my mind, which hardly ever happens. I'm not saying you shouldn't indulge once in a while if you're fit and can afford the extra calories. Life is short and you should enjoy yourself. I'm only suggesting you be aware of the unintended consequences of letting your guard down. It's not only about the additional calories, but also the downward spiral allowing old habits to temporarily resurface. Remember the war you waged to eliminate them, and don't be naïve to believe they're still not strong. You'll be guarding this door for the rest of your life, and be sure to exercise caution whenever you decide to take a break from your post. Old habits die hard. Never underestimate their power.

"Fat people allow bad-eating habits to rule their lives. Fat losers wage war on their old habits, defeat them, and guard the door so they'll never return."

Critical Thinking Question

ARE YOU AWARE OF THE IMPRESSIVE STRENGTH OF YOUR OLD, DEEPLY INGRAINED HABITS AND THE DANGER THEY POSE TO YOUR NEW ONES?

Action Step

Guard the door of your new habits carefully for the rest of your life and never underestimate the old ones.

LEARNING RESOURCES

- *Die Fat or Get Tough*
  www.diefatbook.com

- *Fatlosers - Mental Toughness for Weight Control*
  www.fatlosers.com

- *177 Mental Toughness Secrets*
  www.mentaltoughnesssecrets.com

- *Coaching 177 Mental Toughness Secrets*
  www.coachingmentaltoughness.com

- *Sex Politics Religion Blog*
  www.sexpoliticsreligionblog.com

- *Mental Toughness Blog*
  www.MentalToughnessBlog.com

- *How Rich People Think*
  www.howrichpeoplethinkbook.com

- *Think Rich Team*
  www.thinkrichteam.com

- *The Making of a Million Dollar Mind*
  www.milliondollarmind.com

- *Mental Toughness Mastery*
  www.mentaltoughnessmastery.com

- *Steve on TV*
  www.SteveonTV.com

- *Mental Toughness University Licensee*

The Mental Toughness Book for Dieters that SHOCKED the World!

As seen on:

The Today Show, Good Morning America, ABC News, FOX, NBC, TBS, CBS, BBC Europe and NBC Australia.

Get Chapters 1-5 for FREE at www.diefatbook.com

Register for this FREE 21-day video coaching course and lose weight now!

Each day for the next 21 days you'll receive an email with a link to your 10-15 minute training video for the day. After you watch the video answer three short questions about how you're feeling about your progress. After 21-days of Mental Toughness Training for weight loss, you'll have the tools you need to go the distance and create the body you desire and deserve. Watch the introduction video above, register for the FREE course and get started now! Your new body and your new life are waiting!

visit www.fatlosers.com

Do You Have What It Takes To Ascend To The Throne Of The World-Class?

Can a person of average intelligence and modest means ascend to the throne of the world class? 177 Mental Toughness Secrets of the World Class, identifies and explains the thought processes, habits, and philosophies of the world's greatest performers... and gives you action steps so you can implement these secrets immediately and get what you want.

People Who Adopt These 177 Mental Toughness Secrets Will Be Propelled To The Top. . .Both Personally And Professionally.

Here's What The World-Class is Saying About This Book:

"I find this book and Steve Siebold's mental toughness process to be life changing and liberating. I had a great personal and professional life before I was introduced to mental toughness. After three years of consecutive training, I have a superior life. Steve Siebold is the master of helping people prepare to win."

– Lou Wood
Region Business Director
Johnson & Johnson/OMP

"If you're interested in jump-starting a journey of personal transformation, pick this book up and dive in anywhere. It's a treasure chest of compelling messages and practical exercises. It's up to you to do the work, but Steve Siebold will point you to all the right launching points."

– Amy Edmondson, Ph.D.
Professor of Business Administration
Harvard Business School

Order by the Case and SAVE 20%
www.mentaltoughnesssecrets.com or call 561-733-9078

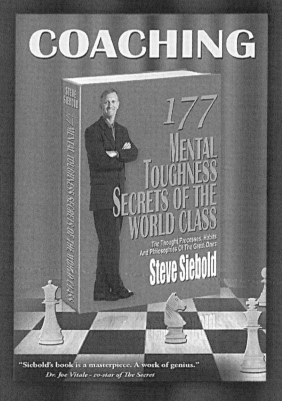

The Video Blog based on the best-selling book hosted by author Steve Siebold. Every week the SPR blog tackles a controversial topic or hot button issue and challenges SPR fans around the world to sound off and state their opinions.

Subscribers include executives, entrepreneurs, politicians, college professors, journalists, thought leaders and concerned citizens worldwide.

All we're missing is YOU!

Get your FREE SUBSCRIPTION at
www.SexPoliticsReligionBlog.com

FREE Video Updates on
MENTAL TOUGHNESS
with Steve Siebold

Join The Discussion! Subscribe Today at

www.MentalToughnessBlog.com

Do You Think Like a Millionaire?

This book will teach you how. It compares the thoughts, habits and philosophies of the middle class to the world class when it comes to wealth. The differences are as extreme as they are numerous. The strategy is simple: learn how rich people think, copy them, take action and get rich This book will teach you how. It compares the thoughts, habits and philosophies of the middle class to the world class when it comes to wealth. The strategy is simple: learn how rich people think, copy them, take action and get rich. If you've ever dreamed of living a life most people only see in movies, study this book like a scientist. Freedom from financial worries and a millionaire's lifestyle is closer than you think.

**How Rich People Think has been featured on
ABC, NBC, CBS, CNBC and the Fox Business Network.**

**GET 5 CHAPTERS FOR FREE AT
www.HowRichPeopleThinkBook.com**

IMAGINE EARNING $100,000/YEAR AS A MENTAL TOUGHNESS COACH FOR WEIGHT-LOSS AND HIGH PERFORMANCE...PART-TIME

70% of Americans are overweight or obese. According to the Center for Disease Control, by 2027, that figure will skyrocket to 90%.

The medical establishment is scrambling for a solution while the government continues try to legislate the problem away.

The Think Rich Team is a trained army of Mental Toughness Coaches around the world solving the problem one client at a time. If you thinkyou have what it takes to become one of our coaches, visit www.fatlosercoach.com

The Making Of A
Million Dollar Mind

"Have You Got What It Takes To Produce

Million Dollar Results?"

For most people, the answer is YES and NO.

YES, they have the POTENTIAL and TALENT.

NO, they lack the BELIEF SYSTEM it takes to ACHIEVE
and SUSTAIN World Class Results.

It's sad, but true.

That's why you see people who have won the lottery losing it,
or getting in trouble with the IRS, or plagued with other self-induced difficulties.

For the top ten distinctions between middle class and world class thinkers visit
www.milliondollarmind.com

MENTAL TOUGHNESS MASTERY
12 CD Series

The great ones believe that nearly any goal is within their reach, and this single belief sets off a mental domino effect that continues to manifest one success after another. They literally THINK their way to the top, and 99% of them are no smarter than you and I.

Here's the problem:
It's not easy to make the distinction between the good and the great unless you know what you're looking for. After 20 years of studying champions, I've discovered that it's really a series of subtleties that add up to make the difference. Without knowing what to look for, most people will completely miss these subtleties. When you stand the champion next to a middle-class performer, there doesn't appear to be much difference. Have you ever thought to yourself, "I can't figure out why so and so is so successful; he/she doesn't seem to be any different than me or anyone else?"

Me, too. But not anymore. The differences are huge, but not very visible. So here's what I've done. I've selected the biggest differences between the winners and the still-trying, and I've put all of this information on a 12 CD series called Mental Toughness Mastery. You will receive 12 CDs detailing exactly how champions think and process information, as well as real life stories and examples of the world-class performers I've worked with over the years, and how to incorporate these ideas and philosophies into your life ... immediately.

Order by calling 561.733.9078 or visit
www.mentaltoughnessmastery.com

FOLLOW STEVE SIEBOLD'S ONGOING TELEVISION APPEARANCES AROUND THE WORLD AT

www.STEVEONTV.com

"IMAGINE YOUR CAREER SPEAKING, TRAINING AND COACHING MENTAL TOUGHNESS/CRITICAL THINKING FOR A LIVING"

The Mental Toughness University Licensee Program offers the unique opportunity to build your business on a foundation of world-class success. If you think you have what it takes to become a successful Mental Toughness Coach, email dawn@ssnlive.org or call 561.733.9078 to receive a no obligation application.

"Becoming a Mental Toughness University Licensee is one the best business decisions I've ever made. I earned $212,000 working part time in the first 18 months"

– Dr. Alok Trivedi, Chicago, Illinois

ABOUT THE AUTHOR

Steve Siebold is a former professional athlete and national coach. He's spent the past 28 years studying the thought processes, habits and philosophies of world class performers. Today he helps Fortune 500 companies increase sales through mental toughness training and critical thinking processes. His clients include Johnson & Johnson, Toyota, and Procter & Gamble. He's written five books on mental toughness with over 200,000 copies in print. He's appeared on The Today Show, Good Morning America, ABC News and dozens of other TV shows around the world. He's quoted regularly in the Wall Street Journal, Fortune, Forbes and numerous other business publications. Steve was named the 2011 Chairman of the National Speakers Associations Million Dollar Speakers Group, which consists of 39 of the wealthiest professional speakers in the world. His numerous television appearances can be seen at www.SteveOnTV.com

Made in the USA
Lexington, KY
13 March 2014